FAMILY SECRETS:
18TH AND 19TH CENTURY BIRTH RECORDS FOUND IN THE WINDHAM COUNTY, CONNECTICUT, COUNTY COURT RECORDS AND FILES AT THE CONNECTICUT STATE LIBRARY ARCHIVES, HARTFORD

I0152782

MARCELLA PASAY

HERITAGE BOOKS
2008

HERITAGE BOOKS
AN IMPRINT OF HERITAGE BOOKS, INC.

Books, CDs, and more—Worldwide

For our listing of thousands of titles see our website
at
www.HeritageBooks.com

Published 2008 by
HERITAGE BOOKS, INC.
Publishing Division
100 Railroad Ave. #104
Westminster, Maryland 21157

Other books by the author:

The Windham County, Connecticut, County Court Records, 1726-1732: Abstracts of Volume I, Connecticut State Library Archives, Capitol Avenue, Hartford, Connecticut
Full Circle: A Directory of Native and African Americans, Windham County, Connecticut, 1650-1900
Windham County, Connecticut, County Court Records, 1732-1736, Abstracts of Volume 2, Connecticut State Library Archives

International Standard Book Numbers
Paperbound: 978-0-7884-1538-5
Clothbound: 978-0-7884-7085-1

This work is dedicated to the staff of the CT State Library & Archives, Historical & Genealogical Division, for their assistance, patience, and encouragement. As caretakers of one of the state's most valuable, and often unrecognized, historical resources, their unfailing devotion to the integrity, protection, maintenance and growth of the collections is to be admired and commended. Thank you.

Table of Contents

Preface

Did you ever wonder as to the reason for the paucity of births in early vital records? Certainly there are many answers to this question--illiteracy, no lawful precedent, and the loss of early books, even if vitals were recorded, just to name a few. Perhaps, if a hint of scandal or embarrassment were associated with a birth, there may have been some reluctance to document it in a public record.

Some say there was no stigma attached to Fornication Before Marriage suits in most cases, and indeed, there might not have been. Melinde Lutz Sanborn in Lost Babes[1] says:

> "In a great majority of cases, fornication did not carry any significant or lasting stigma. If a couple had a child in less than seven months after marriage, they could be fined. This did not usually imply promiscuity, which was handled in another way. A little premarital discovery was hardly rare. In an age when divorce was extremely rare, when marriage was for life, a couple who wanted children wanted to know before they married if they could conceive together."

But what of the single women who bore illegitimate children? Was there a broken promise of marriage by either party? Was she raped? Was he seduced? For as many fornication and maintenance suits as can be found in the court rec-

---

[1]Lost Babes, Fornication Abstracts From Court Records, Essex County, MA, Published Derry, NH, 1992, p. ix

ords there would be an equal number of stories citing some deception or abuse. These events may have caused friction between neighbors and families, especially if the man involved denied his duplicity or the woman made claim against an innocent man. Rumors and scandal may have resulted and some litigants would have fallen into disrepute. This might be something spoken about in whispers and a reason for "family secrets".

There are over three hundred cases in this book, each representing a birth, which, for the most part, is not recorded in the vital records. Previously unpublished marriage dates, names of alleged fathers, some maiden names, and even the names of midwives are revealed. All of these gems were unearthed from the vast treasure chest known as the Windham County, County Court, Records & Files, 1726-1855, (Record Group 3, Main Vault), in the Archives of the CT State Library, Capitol Avenue, Hartford. The value of the Archives and its holdings is priceless and well worth the time extended to plumb its depths.

Introduction

Court Records & Files

The Windham County, County Court, Records & Files, 1726-1855, are stored in two forms. First, records are comprised of thirty-five indexed volumes, thirty-two of which are available to researchers. Volumes seven, eight, and nine are unavailable due to their deteriorated condition. Some of the remaining thirty-two volumes have been refurbished and are divided into three or four parts, separate books, to complete a volume. There are volumes dealing with trials ranging from fornication and maintenance suits, to slander, pleas of debt, highway petitions, assault, theft, contested estates, and even murder, to name just a few. This court also granted licenses to tavern keepers and leather tanners, ferries and fish weirs. Other volumes deal with land executions and still others with defaults.Not all the records are complete but most adhere to an almost standard form, usually a paragraph or two, outlining the major components of a case—the names of the plaintiff and defendant, date of the court, date of the complaint, and the court's findings. When land was involved, in a highway petition or estate case for instance, the property description could cover several pages.

The Files for this series are stored in archival boxes numbered 363 through 518, a total of one hundred fifty five boxes. Files are the paper work generated by a case: Complaints, warrants, summons depositions, expense lists, motions, testimony and case summaries. Not all records are backed up by files and not all files are recorded in volumes one through thirty-five. A number of file boxes were examined in researching this book and any additional data was noted. A few cases, which yielded inordinate amounts of depositions, writs and reports have been highlighted.

Within a number of archival storage boxes file papers are fast deteriorating and lack of funds for restoration may doom them to complete disintegration within a few years. Some document packets are so fragile that they can not be opened for fear they will crumble as the pages are unfolded. Other pages feel damp to the touch even though they are stored within archival boxes in climate controlled conditions.

One box, number 412, is notable because it is almost empty. Only two small packets remain, all that's left of the years 1770 though 1780. There is a note enclosed which explains that the missing files "disappeared" around 1978. One can only hope they were misfiled.

By the time this work is published the Windham County County Court Files may be closed to researchers due to the fragile condition of the Files' contents and lack of funds for preservation will seal their fate.

Fornication & Maintenance Cases

Fornication was illicit sexual intercourse between single persons or a married and unmarried person that resulted in a pregnancy. Fornication before marriage meant that a child was born to a couple less than seven months after the date of their marriage. The majority of suits in this book are fornication, Fornication Before Marriage, and Maintenance. Both types of fornication cases heard before the County Court meant that the birth of a child was imminent or had already taken place. The crime was punishable by a fine or public whipping if the fine could not be paid. The plaintiff in fornication cases was "D. D. Rex", the King, before the American Revolution, or the State of Connecticut beginning in 1783. Someone, usually the King's attorney, or a Justice of the Peace from the local town would file the complaint while the woman was pregnant. She would be summoned to a town Justice Court held in a private home, usually in her town of residence. Depositions from both parties and witnesses would be taken. The presiding Justice of the Peace would then send the case to the County Court to be held after the due date of the child's birth. In Fornication Before Marriage suits the Plaintiff was sometimes the wife, or the husband, or both.

Maintenance, or to be specific, Maintenance of Bastard (language of the Court) cases were brought usually by a single woman against the alleged father of the child. The Plaintiff would be asking the court to require that the Defendant provide support for four years for the child and reimbursement for the expenses of the birth and nursing, plus the court costs. Sometimes, if the girl were a minor, her father would make the Complaint for her. Towns and Boards of Selectmen also served as Plaintiffs for women and children who were paupers. This was not meant as a kindness but for monetary reasons to ensure that the town would not be liable for their support.

Several of the Maintenance suits are featured because of the profusion of paper work found in their files. Using verbatim and abstracted transcriptions are Complaints, Arrest Warrants and Depositions. Together they are a fine example of the workings of the court system of their day and a microcosm of the social and moral structure of early America. To read more on this subject see <u>Sex in Middlesex: Popular Mores in a Massachusetts County, 1649-1699</u>, by Roger Thompson, 1986, University of Massachusetts Press.

When someone acted as surety for either party he was acting as bondsman. It sometimes happened that a person who did not pay his surety would again be called to court for a "Plea of Debt" that could result in an even higher expense because of the additional fine and court costs. There also cases where failure to pay a debt resulted in a jail sentence or "bound" a person to his surety as a servant for a set period of time.

Foreword

Each case is listed alphabetically, by the town of the Plaintiff, and then by the surname of the Plaintiff for Maintenance Cases, or by the town and surname of the Defendant in cases of Fornication. Names with aliases are entered under both names. The date of the writ can be the date of the summons, original complaint, or the Justice of the Peace Court. *All verdicts are guilty unless otherwise noted.*

Every town in Windham County is represented including Lebanon and Mansfield which were later joined with New London and Tolland County, respectively. Border towns such as Tolland and Union, CT, can also be found as well as Dudley, MA, and a few RI neighbors. Several distant towns are named because the Defendants "absconded" rather than face a trial.

A good guideline to estimate a date of birth is that the writs, for the most part, are dated during pregnancy and the County Court date shortly after the birth of the child.

An example of the cases in this work:

D. D. Rex vs. Stephen & Mary Herrick, of Coventry; Fornication (before marriage); County Court June 1727; WCCCR&F, vol. 1 & box 364. Stephen and Mary were married, "the latter end of June or beginning of July, 1726." The child was born 17 October 1726. (Note: The plaintiff in this case was, more specifically, James Fowler, Kings Attorney.)

The plaintiff, defendant(s), and residence are in **bold** print followed by the charge, the County Court date (in some cases the original date of the complaint, or writ, will be listed first) and the abbreviation WCCCR&F (Windham County

County Court Record & Files) with the corresponding volume and file numbers for reference. Some entries will include information from vitals to corroborate with the case information. Abbreviations for town vitals are usually the first letter of the town followed by the letter V except for Coventry (COV), and Pomfret (POV).

ASHFORD, WINDHAM COUNTY, CT

D. D. Rex vs. Esther (Lyon) Abbitt/Abbott, of Ashford; Fornication (before marriage); County Court 25 June 1734; WCCCR, vol. 2.; Nathaniel Abbott, Jr., and Esther Lyon were married 16 April, 1734, in Ashford (AV). Their daughter, Mary was born 22 April 1734 (AV). Nathaniel Abbot, Jr., may have been born 22 May 1714 (AV).

D. D. Rex vs. Hannah Bartholomew, single woman, of Ashford; Fornication; County Court June 1745; WCCCR, vol. 6.

D. D. Rex vs. Mary Carpenter, single woman, of Ashford; Fornication; County Court June 1747; WCCCR, vol. 6.

D. D. Rex vs. Abigail Chaffee, single woman, of Ashford; Fornication; County Court 23 June 1741; WCCCR, vol. 4.

D. D. Rex vs. Abigail Chaffee, single woman, of Ashford; Fornication; County Court December 1760; WCCCF, box 400.

State of Connecticut vs. Sarah Chaffee, single woman, of Ashford; Fornication; County Court December 1802; WCCCR, vol. 20.

State of Connecticut vs. Samuel S. Wright, of Massachusetts; Fornication; County Court March 1829; WCCCR, vol.

29. Found guilty of fornication with Vina Dennis, single
woman, of Ashford, (who was not charged) he was sentenced
to twenty five days in the jail plus court costs. "Vina" may be
Lovian Freeman who married Thomas Dennis 12 April 1822
(AV) and the same "Levina" Dennis who married James Baitan
of New Bedford 20 April 1831 (AV). No death record is
noted for Thomas Dennis however.

D. D. Rex vs. Mary Dexter, single woman, of Ashford;
Fornication; County Court June 1770; WCCCR, vol. 12.

**Mary F. Eastman, single woman, of Ashford vs. Walter
Lyon, of Pomfret**; Maintenance; Justice Court August 1820;
WCCCR, vol. 27; Mary alleges the child was begotten 30 June
1820, in Ashford.

State of Connecticut vs. Polly Ellis, single woman, of
Ashford; Fornication; County Court August 1791; WCCCR,
vol. 18.

D. D. Rex vs. Bashua Fuller, single woman, of Ashford;
Fornication; County Court 24 June 1729; WCCCR, vol. 1.

D. D. Rex vs. Deborah Gold/Gould, of Ashford; Fornication;
County Court 3 June 1751; WCCCF, box 391. According to
the file the child was born before the court date.

D. D. Rex vs. Abigail Gould, single woman, of Ashford; Fornication; Writ 03 March 1778; County Court December 1778; WCCCR, vol. 15.

Hannah Griggs, single woman, of Ashford vs. Erastus Burnham, of Hampton; Maintenance; County Court March 1834; WCCCR, vol. 29. Hannah alleges the male child, begotten 28 November 1832, was born 3 October 1833.

D. D. Rex vs. Lydia Griggs, of Ashford; Fornication; Writ 1 October 1759; County Court February 1760; WCCCF, box 400. "With child" as of the date of the writ. Lydia's surety was Timothy Eastman.

D. D. Rex vs. Ziporah Jugeefor, formerly known as Lysth (Elizabeth) Smith, of Ashford; Fornication; County Court 24 June 1746; WCCCR, vol. 6.

D. D. Rex vs. Abigail Kendall, of Ashford; Fornication; County Court February 1773; WCCCR, vol. 14. Abigail's son, James P-orle (sic), was born 11 November 1773 (AV).

D. D. Rex vs. Isaac & Mary (Chapman) Kendall, of Ashford; Fornication (before marriage); County Court 7 December 1732; WCCCR, vol. 2. Isaac Kendall, Jr., and Mary Chapman were married 15 March 1731/32 (AV); their daughter Mary was born 15 September 1732 (AV). Mary pleads guilty and pays the fine; Isaac pleads not guilty and his case is continued. (Further records not found.) Isaac, Jr., may be the son of Isaac and Hannah born 4 July 1709 (AV).

D. D. Rex vs. Abigail Lee, now of Ashford; Fornication; Writ 5 October 1764; County Court December 1764; WCCCR, vol. 11.

D. D. Rex vs. Abigail Lyon, of Ashford; Fornication; County Court December 1749; WCCCR, vol. 6. The Ashford vitals record the birth of Abigail's son, John Cheney Sumner, 14 April 17--.

Jane Sharer, of Ashford vs. Alexander Ewing, Ashford; Maintenance; Writ 15 April 1731; County Court December 1731; WCCCR, vols. 1 & 2. Alexander is found guilty but Jane appears in court to *not* prosecute her court action. (Note: See Ashford vitals for records of Alexander and *Jean* Ewing.)

D. D. Rex vs. Lysth (Elizabeth) Smith, now known as Ziporah Jugeefor, of Ashford; Fornication; County Court 24 June 1746; WCCCR, vol. 6.

D. D. Rex vs. Keziah Snow, of Ashford; Fornication; County Court February 1767; WCCCR, vol. 11. Keziah's son Shubael was born 23 September 1766 (AV). She may be the daughter of Joseph and Mary Snow born 20 May 1746 (AV). There is a Kezia who married Hubbard Smith (no date) (AV).

State of Connecticut vs. Nehemiah Wade, of Ashford; Fornication; Writ August 1809; County Court August 1809; WCCCR, vol. 21. The alleged crime took place on 2 June 1809 in Ashford with Hannah Brooks, an Indian woman. Hannah was not charged.

State of Connecticut vs. Bethiah Walker, single woman, of Ashford; Fornication; County Court December 1792; WCCCR, vol. 18.

State of Connecticut vs. Laura Wilson, single woman, of Ashford; Secretly Delivered of a Child; County Court August 1836; WCCCR, vol. 29. Court records state that the child was born 19 June 1836 and died shortly after. Laura was fined $100 and sentenced to thirty days in jail. She may be Lorry, daughter of Joseph and Mary Wilson born 3 July 1801 (AV).

Mary Works, of Ashford vs. Edward Keyes, of Ashford; Maintenance; County Court December 1778; WCCCR, vol. 15. Mary could be the daughter of Ingolsbee and Mary Works born 1 January 1759 (AV). Mary and Edward were married 16 June 1779 (AV).

BROOKFIELD[1]

Mercy Davis, of Brookfield vs. Jonathan Shaw, of Woodstock; Maintenance; Writ 18 March 1731; County Court 1731/1732; WCCCR, vol. 1. The records have no further information.

BROOKLYN, WINDHAM COUNTY, CT

Eunice Whitney, of Brooklyn vs. Israel Putnam, 3rd, of Brooklyn; Maintenance; Writ: 08 Dec 1787; County Court August 1788; WCCCR, vol. 17. The child was born in Brooklyn 28 January 1788. The Brooklyn vitals include a Eunice Whitney who married Stephen Backus 2 September 1798.

CANTERBURY, WINDHAM COUNTY, CT

Johannah/Hannah Adams, of Canterbury vs. Ebenezer Baldwin, of Canterbury; Maintenance; County Court 10 Dec 1745; WCCCR, vol. 6. The child, Ebenezer Baldwin, was born 6 April 1745 (BV). John and Esther Adams had a

---

[1]This may be Brookfield, Fairfield County, CT, or Worcester County, MA.

daughter Johannah born 25 April 1712 (CV). Ebenezer is probably the son of John and Mary Baldwin born 14 Oct. 1721 (CV).

D. D. Rex vs. Esther Bates, of Canterbury; Fornication; County Court 28 June 1748; WCCCR, vol. 6. Esther's child, Robert Runnolds, was born 21 February 1748 (CV). The Canterbury vitals include a Robert Runnolds/Reynolds who marries Constance Adams 28 January 1748.

Hannah Bias, Indian woman, of Canterbury vs. John Mulkins, of Canterbury; Maintenance; County Court 22 February 1731/32; WCCCR, vol. 1.

State of Connecticut vs. Abigail Brown, of Canterbury; Fornication; County Court December 1823; WCCCR, vol. 18. The record indicates that Abigail gave birth to a male child begotten before 15 November 1823. Abigail was called three times into court but did not appear.

D. D. Rex vs. Thomas Brown & Elizabeth Cleveland, both of Canterbury; Fornication; County Court 7 February 1736/37; WCCCR, vol. 3. The record states that no one paid the court costs so they must appear at a later date. No other information.

Mehitable Buswell, single woman, of Canterbury vs. Eleazer Cady, of Canterbury; Maintenance; County Court 27 June 1738; WCCCR, vol. 3. The child was born before the court date according to the record but the action was dismissed. Perhaps Eleazer made financial arrangements for the child. Eleazer may be the son of John and Elizabeth Cady born 5 March 1708 (CV). Mehitable Buswell died 16 June 1766 (CV).

D. D. Rex vs. Elizabeth Butts, of Canterbury; Fornication; County Court June 1759; WCCCF, box 399. According to the file the child was born 1 April 1759. Elizabeth could be the daughter of Josiah and Elizabeth (Williams) Butts born 17 February 1735 (CV).

Abigail Cleveland, of Canterbury vs. Benjamin Brown, of Canterbury; Maintenance; Writ 27 April 1732; County Court 1732/1733; WCCCR, vol. 2. Josiah and Abigail (Paine) Cleveland had a daughter Abigail born 3 June 1715 (CV). Benjamin could be the son born 1 September 1713 to Thomas and Rachel (Leavens) Brown. (CV).

Elizabeth Cleveland, of Canterbury vs. Thomas Rose, of Canterbury; Maintenance; Writ 26 December 1741; County Court 22 December 1742; WCCCR, vol. 5.

D. D. Rex vs. Elizabeth Cleveland & Thomas Brown both of Canterbury; Fornication; County Court 7 February 1736/37; WCCCR, vol. 3. The record states that no one paid the court costs so they must appear at a later date. No other information.

State of Connecticut vs. Easter/Esther Cross a.k.a. Esther Hazard, single woman, of Canterbury; Murder; County Court December 1815; WCCCR, vol. 24. The record states that Esther tried to hide her pregnancy but that she gave birth to a child between the 29th and 31st of August 1815. The State contends she carried the murdered infant to Canterbury where she left it on a public highway. She was arrested and sent to jail awaiting trial. Esther was found guilty and fined $50.

D. D. Rex vs. Elizabeth Dixon, single woman, of Canterbury; Fornication; County Court December 1744, 1747, & June 1752; WCCCR&F, vol. 6 & Box 392. Three separate cases of fornication were brought against Elizabeth Dixon "so called". The vital records of Canterbury list four births for Elizabeth Dixon:

       4 June 1743, Mary Gosson/Gibson; died 3 July 1749

       25 May 1747, Edward Gosson/Gibson

       21 February 1752, Ichabod Gosson/Gibson

       30 December 1753 Mary Cammel/Campbell

Abigail Downing, of Canterbury vs. William Huntington, of Mansfield; Maintenance; Writ 07 July 1778; County Court December 1778; WCCCR, vol. 15. The records divulge that the child was born 20 November 1778 in Canterbury. The defendant did not appear.

D. D. Rex vs. Catherine Downing, of Canterbury; Fornication; County Court June 1760; WCCCF, box 400. Catherine's child was born 29 March 1759. John Ormsby was Catherine's surety.

D. D. Rex vs. Elizabeth Durfy/Durby, single woman, of Canterbury; Fornication; County Court June 1779; WCCCR, vol. 15. Elizabeth Durfy had son Jedediah born 22 October 1778 (CV). Benjamin and Elizabeth (Downing) Durfy had a daughter Elizabeth born 26 July 1758.

State of Connecticut vs. Tryphena Durfey, of Canterbury; Fornication; Writ 11 September 1782 (1st case); County Courts June 1783 & August 1789; WCCCR, vols. 16 & 17. Two separate cases are recorded. Canterbury vitals note the birth of a daughter, Elizabeth Allen, on 3 July 1782. The court records disclose yet another birth in August 1788. Tryphena may be the daughter of Benjamin and Elizabeth Durfey born 17 February 1760 (CV).

John Francis, of Canterbury, for his daughter Harriet, a minor vs. Samuel S. Cotton, of Pomfret; Maintenance; County Court August 1841; WCCCR, vol. 31. The child, begotten 1 August 1840, was born 22 April 1841. Harriet could be the woman who married Luther Sanger 7 June 1847 (CV).

Sarah Gibbins/Gibson/Gosson, of Canterbury vs. Jonathan Carver, of Canterbury; Maintenance; County Court 24 June 1729; WCCCR, vol. 1.

State of Connecticut vs. Elizabeth Green, of Canterbury; Fornication; County Court August 1785; WCCCR, vol. 16. Her son Jonathan Fairle Rue was born 2 December 1784 (CV); a daughter Petifeel Pierpont Phillips born on 1 April 1791 (CV).

D. D. Rex vs. Eunice Green, of Canterbury; Fornication; County Courts June 1771 & June 1779; WCCCR, vols. 12 & 15. Eunice did not appear for either one of these cases. Her son Alanson was born 12 June 1784, and son Rule was born 5 August 1788 according to the Canterbury vitals.

State of Connecticut vs. Esther/Easter Hazard a.k.a. Esther Cross, single woman, of Canterbury; Murder; County Court December 1815; WCCCR, vol. 24. The record states that Esther tried to hide her pregnancy but that she gave birth to a child between the 29th and 31st of August 1815. The

State contends she carried the murdered infant to Canterbury where she left it on a public highway. She was arrested and sent to jail awaiting trial. Esther was found guilty and fined $50.

State of Connecticut vs. Mehitable Knapping, of Canterbury; Fornication; County Court August 1785; WCCCR, vol. 16.

D. D. Rex vs. Mary Manning, of Canterbury; Fornication; County Court February 1747/48; WCCCR, vol. 6.

D. D. Rex vs. Hannah Rude/Rood, of Canterbury; Fornication; County Court 23 June 1741; WCCCR, vol. 4.

Lucy Shepard, single woman, of Canterbury vs. Deliverance Woodward, of Canterbury; Maintenance; Writ 10 June 1737; County Court 21 June 1738; WCCCR, vol. 3. The record discloses the child's birth as 21 June 1737. Woodward, the defendant, did not appear. Deliverance is probably the son of John and Hannah Woodward born 5 November 1713 (CV), who marries Abigail Juel 7 March 1737 (CV).

Sela Spalding, of Canterbury vs. John Felch, of Canterbury; Maintenance; Writ 6 August 1791; County Court August 1791; WCCCR, vol. 18. Twins were born 24 May 1791 in Canterbury. The case is dropped because Sela has received compensation from John Felch. John is probably the son of John and Sarah (Adams) Felch born 24 July 1770 (CV). There is also a marriage for a John Felch to Eunice Baldwin on 12 April 1796 (CV).

Mary Spaulding, single woman, of Canterbury vs. Isaac Adams, of Canterbury; Maintenance; Writ 13 July 1726; County Court 20 December 1728; WCCCR&F, vol. 1 & box 363. The file reveals that the child was born "near" 14 July 1726 and that Mary is the daughter of Lieutenant Samuel Spaulding, deceased. She is probably the Mary born to Samuel and Mary Spaulding 2 March 1710 (CV). Isaac Adams may have married Gerviah/Zerviah Brown 17 February 1728/29 (CV).

D. D. Rex vs. Amey Stanton, single woman of Canterbury; Fornication; Writ 10 July 1761; County Court December 1761; WCCCF, box 401. Amon (Amos?) was born to Amey 27 June 1761. Witnesses to the birth were the wife of Jacob Staples and the wife of Nathan Goram. The Canterbury vitals record five births for Amey Stanton:

> Abiah, daughter born 14 November 175-
> Amon/Amis, son born 27 June 17--
> Hosea, son born 27 June 17--
> Content, daughter born 12 July 17--
> Joel, son born 16 August 17--.

D. D. Rex vs. Sarah Stanton, single woman, of Canterbury; Fornication; County Court December 1758; WCCCF, box 398. The child was born 19 July 1758.

D. D. Rex vs. Elizabeth Thatcher, of Canterbury; Fornication; County Court 23 June 1741; WCCCR, vol. 4. Elizabeth's surety was Benajah Douglass.

State of Connecticut vs. Lucy Wilkenson, of Canterbury; Fornication; County Court December 1783; WCCCR, vol. 16. There is a Lucy Wilkenson born to Sarah Lombard May 26 1751 (CV). Lucy may have married Nathaniel Smith 8 September 1784 (CV).

D. D. Rex vs. Abigail Williams, of Canterbury; Fornication; County Court 24 June 1776; WCCCR, vol. 6. Isaiah and Abigail (Knight) Williams had daughter Abigail born 22 August 1745 (CV).

CHAPLIN, WINDHAM COUNTY, CT

Selectmen of the Town of Chaplin for Melinda Coburn, of Chaplin vs. Andrew Hartshorn, of Hampton; Maintenance; County Court March 1824; WCCCR, vol. 28. The child, a female, was begotten in Hampton on 19 March 1823 and born there 19 December 1823 according to the court record. See Hampton vitals for Andrew Hartshorn.

COLUMBIA, TOLLAND COUNTY, CT

State of Connecticut vs. James Freeman, of Columbia; Fornication; County Court March 1811; WCCCR, vol. 23. The alleged crime took place with Theodora Convonant, a single woman, of Columbia, who was not charged. Found guilty, James is whipped ten stripes and fined.

Amanda Little, of Columbia vs. Stephen Hosmer, of Columbia; Maintenance; County Courts August 1816 & August 1818; WCCCR, vol. 13 & 24. The child was born 13 June 1816. In 1818 Stephen brings a suit against Amanda and Jonah Hutchinson claiming he is not guilty of the 1816 charge. No decision was made on the new case. Further information was unavailable.

COVENTRY, TOLLAND COUNTY, CT

Rachel Davenport, of Coventry vs. Dennis Parker, of Coventry; Maintenance; County Court June 1772; WCCCR, vol. 13. Rachel's child, also named Dennis Parker, was born 17 April 1772 (COV). There is a Rachel, daughter of Richard and Elies Davenport born 2 March 1745 (COV). Dennis Parker born 12 January 1742/43 is the son of Phineas and Martha (Meraugh) Parker (COV).

D. D. Rex vs. Joseph & Joanna Davis, of Coventry; Fornication (before marriage); County Court 25 June 1728;
WCCCR, vol. 1. Their first child Joseph was born 18 August
1727 and their second, Irene, was born 1 May 1728, before the
County Court date.

**D. D. Rex vs. Elisha Fitch and "his now wife" Priscilla
(Patten), of Coventry;** Fornication (before marriage); County
Court 14 December 1736; WCCCR, vol. 3. Elisha and Priscilla
were married 27 May 1736 (COV). Deborah, their daughter,
was born 5 July 1736 (COV).

**Martha Grant, of Coventry vs. Amos Thompson, of Cov-
entry;** Maintenance; County Court June 1748; WCCCR, vol.
6. Martha's child was born 15 February 1748. The Coventry
vitals tell us that an Amos Thompson married Irane Dodge 17
May 1750 (COV).

D. D. Rex vs. Mary Harrington, of Coventry; Fornication;
Writ 6 January 1772; County Court June 1773; WCCCR, vol.
14.

**Mary Hendee, single woman, of Coventry vs. (Dr.) Henry
Ladd, of Coventry;** Maintenance; County Court June 1772;
WCCCR, vol. 13. The child, Silenda, was begotten May,
1771, and born 10 February 1772 (COV). Mary may be the

daughter of Asa and Mary Hendee born 14 January 1751 (COV).

D. D. Rex vs. Stephen & Mary Herrick, of Coventry; Fornication (before marriage); County Court June 1727; WCCCR&F, vol. 1 & box 364. Stephen and Mary were married, "the latter end of June or beginning of July, 1726." The child was born 17 October 1726. (Note: The plaintiff in this case was, more specifically, James Fowler, Kings Attorney.)

D. D. Rex vs. Martha Millington, of Coventry; Fornication; County Courts June 1729 & 7 December 1732; WCCCR, vols. 1 & 2. Two separate cases of fornication were entered into the records. Martha may be the daughter of John and Martha Millington born March 1706/07 (COV).

D. D. Rex vs. Ruth Peters, of Coventry; Fornication; County Court June 1772 & August 1780; WCCCR, vols. 13 & 215. Two separate cases of fornication were entered into the records. No other information recorded.

D. D. Rex vs. Susannah Porter, of Coventry; Fornication; County Court 23 June 1741; WCCCR, vol. 4.

Anne Richardson, of Coventry vs. Nathaniel Thompson, of Coventry; Maintenance; County Court June 1778; WCCCR, vol. 15. The record states that the child was begotten 26 January 1777 and born August 1777. Anne is probably the daughter of Amos, Jr., and Ruth (Stiles) Richardson born 26 March 1752 (COV). Nathaniel may be the son of Nathaniel and Hannah (Dodge) Thompson born 15 March 1753 (COV).

Jane Robinson, of Coventry vs. William Taylor, of Coventry; Maintenance; County Court 23 June 1741; WCCCR, vol. 4.

D. D. Rex vs. Samuel & Mercy (Parker) Root, of Coventry; Fornication (before marriage); County Court December 1729; WCCCR, vol. 1. The Coventry vitals provide us with the following: Samuel Root and Mercy Parker were married 12 March 1728/29; Samuel, son of Samuel and Mercy born 26 August 1729. Samuel (Sr.'s) birth record is perhaps the Samuel born 17 October 1705 from those "records from Northampton" in the Coventry vitals.

D. D. Rex vs. (Dr.) Josiah & Eunice (Meecham) Rose, of Coventry; Fornication (before marriage); County Court December 1739; WCCCR, vol. 3. Josiah, their son, was born 5 July 1739 (COV). Josiah and Eunice were married 9 May 1739 (COV). Eunice may be the daughter of Rev. Joseph and Esther (Coy) Meecham born 25 May 1716 (COV).

D. D. Rex vs. Chloe Rust, of Coventry; Fornication; County Court June 1769; WCCCR, vol. 12. See Coventry vitals. Elizabeth Scripture, daughter of Cloe Rust, was born 23 November 1768 (COV).

D. D. Rex vs. Noah & Keziah (Strong) Rust, of Coventry; Fornication (before marriage); County Court 25 June 1728; WCCCR&F, vol. 1 & box 364. The testimony of a witness, Elizabeth Lee, was included in the files. Lee states that Keziah Rust was suspected of being with child before marriage by both mothers-in law and "several other" people. According to the file Keziah was four months and four days married when she became ill and in "travill" (travail, or labor). (Coventry vitals record their marriage as 2 November 1727.) Elizabeth Lee, of Coventry, who is most likely a midwife, asked Keziah repeatedly if she was with child before marriage and Keziah replied "No" every time. The child was stillborn, the body about twelve to fourteen inches long, "very much bruised" and the skin came off in several places. Keziah testified that she felt the child stir two or three days before the birth. Mary Rust (probably Noah's mother), who was also present at the birth, swore that it looked as if the child had been dead some time before birth. Verdict: Not guilty.

D. D. Rex vs. Abigail Simons/Simonds, of Coventry; Fornication; County Court December 1765; WCCCR, vol. 11.

Elizabeth Washburn, single woman, of Coventry vs. Henry Ladd, of Coventry; Maintenance; County Court December 1772; WCCCR, vol. 13. The child, named Phillip N. Ladd, was begotten 25 September 1771 and according to the Coventry vitals born 16 June 1772. Henry is probably the son of Henry and Abigail (Liley) Ladd born 25 January 1742/43 (COV).

ENFIELD, HARTFORD COUNTY, CT

Jemima Meechum, of Enfield vs. Nathaniel Bassett, Jr., of Mansfield; Maintenance; Writ 10 March 1731/32; County Court 1732; WCCCR, vol. 2. Jemima's child, Dorcas Bassett was born 13 November 1731 (EV). The parties reappeared in court in December 1732 but the original verdict of "guilty" held.

HAMPTON, WINDHAM COUNTY, CT

Anna Curtis, of Hampton vs. Samuel Spalding, of Hampton; Maintenance; Writ November 1790; County Court 15 February 1791; WCCCR, vol. 18. Anna gave birth to Samuel Spalding, Jr., on 15 October 1790 (HV). Anna is probably the daughter of John and Hannah (Mosely) Curtis born 24 December 1767 (HV). Samuel may have married Mercy Starkweather 24 February 1811 HV).

Lois/Louis Durgee/Durkee/Darby, of Hampton vs.
Ebenezer Griffin, of Hampton; Maintenance; County Court
August 1797; WCCCR, vol. 18. Ebenezer Griffin and Lois
Darbee/Durkee? were married 1 January 1804 (HV).
Louis/Lois Darbe, born 16 June 1777, daughter of Andrew and
Mary (Benjamin) Darbe (This should be "Durkee" according to
Bernice Gunderson, a Durkee descendant.).

Nancy Linkon/Lincoln, of Hampton vs. George Robinson,
of Windham; Maintenance; County Court August 1804;
WCCCR, vol. 20. The records state that the child was begotten on 6 March 1803 and born 13 January 1804 in Hampton.

Olive Martin, single woman, of Hampton vs. Christopher
Maynard, of Waterford; Maintenance; Writ 23 August 1806;
County Court December 1806; WCCCR&F, vol. 21 & box
440. Olive's child was born 17 October 1806 according to the
files. The Hampton vitals state that Olive gave birth to a
daughter, Mary Minor (Maynard?), on 16 October 1806. (A
Mary Ann Minor died 11 September 1832 (HV). There is also
another birth and a possible marriage for Olive in the Hampton
vitals to Samuel Davison of Plainfield, MA, 14 January 1823.
Olive may be the daughter of Nathaniel Ford and Jerusha
(Linkon) Martin, born 27 September 1784 (HV). Documents
for Martin vs. Maynard included the following :
- A copy of the original Complaint and Warrant: Olive
  Martin, the Plaintiff, a single woman, of Hampton, first
  brings her complaint to Philip Pearl, Justice of the Peace in

Hampton. She says that she became pregnant about the first of March 1806. He hears her complaint and issues a warrant for the arrest of Christopher Maynard, Jr., of Waterford, August 23 1806. The Justice Court is held in Hampton. Both parties appear and Maynard pleads not guilty. The Court orders Maynard to procure a bond of two hundred dollars and appear before Windham County Court the first Tuesday of December 1806. Some of the expenses and fees are listed to total $4.02. The bottom half seems to be part of the Windham County Court Record reviewing the Complaint and adding that Olive Martin gave birth to her child 17 October 1806. The last page again states the plea of not guilty by Christopher Maynard. The verdict can be interpreted as guilty because the terms of maintenance payments are listed (upside-down under the names of the Plaintiff and Defendant). Total court fees and expenses total $31.77. Signed L. Ingals.

- A copy of the original bond statement made by Christopher Maynard dated 27 August 1806 and witnessed by Andrew Maynard and Gracy Maynard. It was also certified by Philip Pearl, Justice of the Peace. An arrest warrant dated 17 January 1807. The Sheriff of New London County is directed to go to Waterford, find Christopher Maynard, and recover support payments for the child and payable to Olive Martin. The total, so far, owed Olive is $40.48, plus 17 cents for the cost of the writ. The Sheriff is ordered to put Maynard in jail until he pays what is due. Signed Samuel Gray, Clerk (of the Court).
- A report dated 4 February 1807 certifies that the Deputy was unable to locate the debtor Christopher Maynard within his precinct. The "Execution Granted August 28, 1807" might mean the court formally pursued a case against Maynard to recover costs and maintenance. Signed Henry Webb, Deputy Sheriff.

Selectmen of Hampton for Clarissa Neff, of Hampton vs. Jesse Fuller, of Brooklyn; Maintenance; County Court December 1821; WCCCR, vol. 27. Clarissa's child was born 23 October 1819, in Hampton. The case was dismissed.

Phebe Upton, of Hampton vs. Andrew Hartshorn, of Hampton; Maintenance; County Court December 1796; WCCCR, vol. 18. The child was born 21 June 1796. Andrew Hartshorn may have married twice--but not to Phebe Upton. (See HV).

KILLINGLY, WINDHAM, COUNTY, CT

D. D. Rex vs. Rachel Brooks, of Killingly; Fornication; Writ 10 April 1758; County Court June 1759; WCCCF, box 399. Rachel's child was born in January 1759. Her surety was John Brooks.

D. D. Rex vs. Elizabeth Brown, single woman, of Killingly; Fornication; County Courts 22 June 1736, 22 June 1742 & June 1759 ; WCCCR&F, vol. 2 & 5 & box 399. Three separate cases. The date of birth for one of the children is given as September 1758. Surety for Elizabeth in 1759 was Stephen Brown.

Abigail Cady, of Killingly vs. Samuel Brown, of Pomfret; Maintenance; Writ 5 December 1782; County Court June 1783

& February 1785; WCCCR, vol. 16. The unnamed child was born 4 December 1782, in Killingly. After two trials Samuel Brown was found not guilty.

Prudence Cay/Cady, of Killingly vs. Jesse Cady, of Scituate, RI; Maintenance; Writ 22 December 1769; County Court June 1769; WCCCR, vol. 12. The Cady child was born 26 March 1770 according to the court record. Prudence may be the daughter of Jonathan and Betty Cady born 20 April 1750 (KV). Jesse is possibly the son of Barnabas and Margaret born 10 April 1752 (KV), in which case both Prudence and Jesse are twins.

Ruth Converse, of Killingly vs. Samuel Carpenter, of Pomfret; Maintenance; County Court 23 June 1741; WCCCR, vol. 4. The record states the child was born before the court date. Surety for Samuel was Dr. John Hallowell. Ruth is probably the daughter of Samuel and Hannah Converse, born 28 May 1718 (KV).

Abigail Cooper, of Killingly vs. Comfort Eaton, of Killingly; Maintenance; Writ 20 April 1750; County Court December 1750; WCCCR, vol. 6. Court papers declare the child was begotten October 1749 and the Killingly vitals tells us that Comfort Eaton was born to Abigail on 22 June 1750. Abigail is probably the daughter of Timothy and Sarah Cooper born 13 March 1730/31 (KV).

D. D. Rex vs. Samuel & Sarah (Cooper) Daily, of Killingly;
Fornication (before marriage); County Court 27 June 1727;
WCCCR, vol. 1. The court alleges that the child was born
"near four months after marriage". Their son Samuel, Jr., was
born 29 June 1726 (KV), the date of marriage being 3 March
1726.

D. D. Rex vs. Mehittable Elltrip/Elliothorpe, of Killingly;
Fornication; County Court 22 June 1742; WCCCR, vol. 5.

**Sarah Farmon/Fairman, single woman, of Killingly vs.
John Russell, of Killingly**; Maintenance; 15 July 1728;
WCCCF, box 365. Sarah is "with child" at the time of the
court date. Her father John Fairman is her surety.

**Mary Heffernon (alias Russell), of Killingly vs. Samuel
Lawrence, of Killingly**; Maintenance; County Court June
1730; WCCCR&F, vol. 1, box 367. The charges state that the
child was born 25 February 1729/30. David Russell (Samuel's
stepfather) was surety for both Mary and Samuel. See next
case.

**Mary Heffernon (alias Russell), of Killingly vs. John Priest,
of Killingly**; Maintenance; Writ 7 November 1732; County
Court 1733/34; WCCCR, vol. 2. No one appeared. Case
dismissed. John Priest married Peggy Dugles 5 November
1734 (KV).

D. D. Rex vs. Olive Herrington, single woman, of Killingly;
Fornication; County Court December 1758; WCCCF, box 398.
The file papers report the child's birth as June or July 1758.
The witnesses, all of Killingly, were: Dorothy Herrington,
Elizabeth Whitmore and Abigail Robins.

**Elizabeth Leavens, single woman, of Killingly vs. Timothy
Cutler, of Killingly**; Maintenance; Writ 27 September 1737;
County Court 1738/1739; WCCCR, vol. 3. The child, Benoni
Cutler, was born 17 August 1737 (KV).

**Mehitable Morris, of Killingly vs. (Dr.) John Hallowell, a
transient person**; Maintenance; County Court 13 December
1726; WCCCR&F, vol. 1 & box 363. Mehitable alleges that
the child was begotten 1 January 1726 and born in October
1726. Hallowell absconded to Middletown (Middlesex
County, CT). Mehitable's surety was Benjamin Morris and her
witness was Samuel Morris, Jr. (Note: John Hallowell is involved in a number of lawsuits during this time period, both as
a plaintiff and a defendant--many are "pleas of debt".) There
are birth records of children to parents "John and Mehetable
Hallowell" in the Killingly vitals but a marriage is not recorded
for Morris and Hallowell. Benjamin Morris names one of his
sons "John Hallowell Morris".

**Elizabeth Preston, single woman, of Killingly vs. William
Jarvis, of Killingly**; Maintenance; County Court 12 September 1726; WCCCR&F, vol. 1, box 363 & 364. Elizabeth al-

leges the child was begotten 30 June 1726. Samuel Lee was surety for Elizabeth. Both parties defaulted on their appearances.

D. D. Rex vs. Anna Randall, single woman, of Killingly; Fornication; County Court December 1761 ; WCCCF, box 401. Anna's daughter was born the "latter end" of February 1761. Witnesses were Sarah Cooper (the midwife), and Abi Brown, wife of Nathaniel. Surety for Anna was Stephen Brown.

Mary Russell (alias Heffernon), of Killingly vs. Samuel Lawrence, of Killingly; Maintenance; County Court June 1730; WCCCR&F, vol. 1, box 367. The charges state that the child was born child was born 25 February 1729/30. David Russell (Samuel's stepfather) was surety for both Mary and Samuel. See next case.

Mary Russell (alias Heffernon), of Killingly vs. John Priest, of Killingly; Maintenance; Writ 7 November 1732; County Court 1733/34; WCCCR, vol. 2. No one appeared. Case dismissed. John Priest married Peggy Dugles 5 November 1734 (KV).

Lorena Sparks, of Killingly vs. John Smith, of Killingly; Maintenance; County Court August 1797; WCCCR, vol. 18. Lorena's child was born 2 July 1797.

D. D. Rex vs. Hannah, wife of Edward Stewart, of Killingly; Fornication (before marriage); County Court 9 December 1735; WCCCR, vol. 2. Their daughter Mary Stewart was born 29 June 1735 (KV).

D. D. Rex vs. Sarah Sweeney, single woman, of Killingly; Fornication; County Court 9 December 1740; WCCCR, vol. 4.

Mary Utter, of Killingly vs. Jonathan Waldo, of Pomfret, absconded to Providence, RI; Maintenance; Writ 7 February 1750/51; Court 22 June 1751; WCCCR, vol. 6. According to the court records the child was begotten July 1750. The birth of Abigail Walder/Waldo is listed in the Killingly vitals as 4 April 1751. Witnesses who attended the birth at Samuel Utter's in Killingly were: Deborah (possibly Dorothy, wife of Luther) Torrey, Hulda Johnson, and Johanna Utter, all of Killingly. Mary may be the daughter of Samuel and Johannah Utter born 30 March 1725 (KV).

LEBANON, NEW LONDON COUNTY, CT

D. D. Rex vs. Hannah Armstrong, of Lebanon; Fornication; County Court 12 December 1738; WCCCR, vol. 3.

D. D. Rex vs. Desire Bartlett, of Lebanon; Charge Fornication; County Court June 1748; WCCCR, vol. 6. There are birth records for the children of "Ichabod and Desire Bartlett" in the Lebanon vitals.

D. D. Rex vs. Martha Bill, of Lebanon; Fornication; County Court December 1768 WCCCR, vol. 12. Martha may be the daughter of John and Mary Bill born 23 October 1743 (LV).

D. D. Rex vs. Mehitable (Dowey) Bill, wife of Jonathan, of Lebanon; Fornication (before marriage) County Court December 1752; WCCCF, box 392. Jonathan Bill and Mehitable Dowey were married 26 August 1751. Their child was born the end of February or early March 1752. Witnesses called: Hannah Bliss and Sarah Loomis, both of Lebanon.

D. D. Rex vs. Zerviah, wife of Elias Bliss, of Lebanon; Fornication (before marriage); Writ 13 August 1755; County Court June 1756; WCCCF, box 396. Zerviah and Elias were married 31 December 1754 and their child was born 5 June 1755. Witnesses called: The wife of Thomas Loomis, the wife of Thomas Loomis, Jr., and the wife of Stephen Strong, all of Lebanon. Elias is probably the son of Henry and Bethiah Bliss born 9 February 1733 (LV).

D. D. Rex vs. Lois Bradford alias Ramont(Raymond?), of Lebanon; Fornication; Writ 18 June 1750; County Court December 1750; WCCCR, vol. 6.

D. D. Rex vs. Keziah Brewster, of Lebanon; Fornication;
County Court June 1745; WCCCR, vol. 6.

D. D. Rex vs. Beulah Briscoe, of Lebanon; Fornication; Writ
June 1748; County Court December 1750; WCCCR, vol. 6.

D. D. Rex vs. Nancy Clark, single woman, of Lebanon;
Fornication; Writ 4 May 1761; County Court June 1761;
WCCCF, box 401. The child was born the 20th of (page torn)
1761. Witness: The wife of Lieutenant Ezekiel Fitch.

D. D. Rex vs. Hannah (Brewster) Crandall, wife of Constant, of Lebanon; Fornication (before marriage); Writ 4 October 1743; County Court 13 December 1743; WCCCR, vol.
5. Hannah was probably the daughter of William and Mehitable Brewster born 31 March 1718 (LV). She married Constant Crandall 18 May 1743 (LV). Acting as Surety for Hannah were her husband Constant and Gershom Mattoon. No
one appeared in court.

D. D. Rex vs. Samuel & Ann Buell, of Lebanon; Fornication
(before marriage); County Court 24 June 1729; WCCCR, vol.
1. Samuel could be the son of William and Elizabeth Buell
born 5 November 1708 (LV).

D. D. Rex vs. Sybil Chappel, single woman, of Lebanon.
There are five separate cases of fornication in which Sybil is a

litigant. In the first three she is the defendant; In the last two she is the plaintiff: Fornication; County Court February 1747, February 1749, December 1750 & October 1752 ; WCCCR&F, vol. 6 & box 392. One of Sybil's children was born about the middle of June 1752. She was arrested on the charge of not paying her fine for fornication. Witnesses called for the birth of the child were Mary and Martha Vaughn of Lebanon. Sybil escaped from jail in December, was apprehended, and in March 1753 sentenced to be "whipped seven stripes on her naked body" at the public whipping post in Windham.

Sybil Chappel, single woman, of Lebanon vs. Elijah Bill, of Lebanon; Maintenance; County Court June 1758; WCCCF, box 398. Sybil is "with child" at the time of the court proceedings. No one appeared.

Sybil Chappel, single woman, of Lebanon vs. Joseph Brown, of Lebanon; Maintenance; Writ December 1765; County Court June 1766; WCCCR, vol. 11. Sybil's child was born 10 August 1765.

D. D. Rex vs. Grace, wife of Joseph Clarke, Jr., of Lebanon; Fornication (before marriage); County Court June 1758; WCCCR, vol. 3.

D. D. Rex vs. Jerusha Crane, of Lebanon; Fornication; County Court June 1745 & June 1748; WCCCR, vol. 6. These are two separate cases. The Lebanon vitals record the marriage of Jerusha Crane and Lemuel Crane 13 May 1757 (LV).

Mary Crane, of Lebanon vs. Timothy Buel, of Lebanon; Maintenance; County Court 23 June 1730; WCCCR, vol. 1. Timothy may be the son of William Buel born 24 October 1711 (LV).

D. D. Rex vs. Hezekiah Culver, of Lebanon; Fornication; County Court December 1750; WCCCR, vol. 6.

D. D. Rex vs. Sarah Cutting, of Lebanon; Fornication; County Court 26 June 1744; WCCCR, vol. 5.

Hannah Davis, of Lebanon vs. Andrew Dewey, of Lebanon; Maintenance; County Court June 1773; WCCCR, vol. 14. The record tells us that the male child was begotten in May 1772 and born 11 February 1773. Hannah was probably the daughter of Samuel and Alice (Swift) Davis who was born 21 January 1754 (LV). Andrew may have been born 29 December 1751, son of Solomon and Anne (Downer) Dewey (LV).

Hannah Davis, of Lebanon vs. Augustus Wheatlock Bingham, of Lebanon; Maintenance; Writ 21 April 1783; County Court June 1783; WCCCR, vol. 16. Twins were born to Hannah on 12 May 1783 in Lebanon.

Submit Dewey, of Lebanon vs. Phineas Sprague. of Lebanon; Maintenance; Writ 2 December 1773; County Court December 1773; WCCCR, vol. 14. Submit was probably the daughter of Abraham and Grace (Gates) Dewey born 27 October 1756 (LV).

D. D. Rex vs. Silence (How) Fitch, wife of Azel, of Lebanon; Fornication (before marriage); Writ 3 October 1752; County Court December 1752; WCCCF, box 392. Azel and Silence were married 1 January 1752 and their child was born between the 26th and 30th of July 1752. Azel may be the son of Joseph and Ann Fitch born 7 November 1726 (LV).

D. D. Rex vs. Susannah, wife of Ezekiel Fitch, of Lebanon; Fornication (before marriage); County Court June 1749; WCCCR, vol. 6

D. D. Rex vs. Abigail Fowler, of Lebanon; Fornication; Writ 18 October 1764; County Court December 1764; WCCCR, vol. 11. In the Lebanon vitals there is an Abigail born 1 March 1747 to Dijah and Abigail (Bigelow) Fowler.

D. D. Rex vs. Philip & wife Margaret Gay, of Lebanon; Fornication (before marriage); County Court 10 December 1734; WCCCR, vol. 2. Eleanor, daughter of Philip and Margaret, born 6 May 1734 (LV).

D. D. Rex vs. Sarah Gay, of Lebanon; Fornication; County Court 26 June 1733; WCCCR, vol. 2.

D. D. Rex vs. Elizabeth Graves, of Lebanon; Fornication; County Court 9 December 1748; WCCCR, vol. 4.

Priscilla Green, of Lebanon vs. Ichabod Warner, Jr., of Lebanon; Maintenance; Writ 10 December 1733; County Court 6 February 1733/34; WCCCR, vol. 2. Ichabod is perhaps the son of Ichabod and Mary (Metcalf) Warner born 10 December 1712 (LV).

D. D. Rex vs. Phebe Greenman, late of Stonington, now of Lebanon; Fornication; County Court June 1746; WCCCR, vol. 6.

D. D. Rex vs. Bartholomew & Eleoner (Corbit) Heath, of Lebanon; Fornication (before marriage); County Court 24 June 1735; WCCCR, vol. 2. From the Lebanon vitals we learn that they were married 3 October 1734 and their son Joseph Heath was born 22 April 1735.

D. D. Rex vs. Mary House, of Lebanon; Fornication; County Court 23 June 1741; WCCCR, vol. 4.

D. D. Rex vs. Esther, wife of Ezekiel Huntington, of Lebanon; Fornication (before marriage); County Court December 1758; WCCCR, vol. 4. Joseph probably son of Ezekiel Huntington, born 25 May 1758 (LV).

D. D. Rex vs. May/Mary (Wattle) Hyde/Hide, wife of Daniel, of Lebanon; Fornication (before marriage); County Court June 1761; WCCCF, box 401. Mary and Daniel were married in November 1760. Their child was born 25 January 1761.

Margaret Johnson, single woman, of Lebanon vs. John Foster, a transient; Maintenance; County Court December 1752; WCCCF, box 392. Margaret's child was born 26 February 1752. Witnesses to the birth were Mary Dana and Mindwell (Tisdale) Fitch of Lebanon. Margaret may be the daughter of William and Mary Johnson born 14 December 1716 (LV).

D. D. Rex vs. Mary (Brewster), wife of John Johnson, Jr., of Lebanon; Fornication (before marriage); County Court June 1749; WCCCR, vol. 6. The marriage is noted in the Lebanon vitals without a date. Mary, daughter of John and Mary Johnson was born 27 November 1748 (LV).

D. D. Rex vs. Mabel Little, of Lebanon; Fornication; Writ 21
June 1772; County Court June 1774; WCCCR, vol. 14.
Surety for Mabel was Ichabod Robinson. Mabel could be the
daughter of Nathaniel and Mabel Little born 2 February 1750
(LV).

D. D. Rex vs. Esther Loomis, of Lebanon; Fornication ;
County Court 24 February 1735/36; WCCCR, vol. 2.

**D. D. Rex vs. Alice (Newcomb) Marsh, wife of Jonathan
Marsh, of Lebanon;** Fornication (before marriage); County
Court 9 December 1735; WCCCR, vol. 2. The marriage of
Alice and Jonathan Marsh is noted in the Lebanon vitals with-
out a date. Their daughter Elizabeth was born 26 July 1735
(LV). Alice is probably the daughter of John and Alice New-
comb born 24 March 1712 (LV). Jonathan may be the son of
Joseph and Hannah Marsh born 23 September 1713(LV).

**State of Connecticut vs. Thankful (Lyman) Mowrey, of
Lebanon;** Fornication; Writ; 6 April 1796; County Court 12
August 1796; WCCCR&F, vol. 18 & box 426. Thankful's
child was born 7 January 1796. There is a Thankful Smith
Lyman, daughter of Caleb & Mary (Bettis) Lyman, born 13
May 1766 (LV). Documents in the file included:
• The Complaint against Thankful, now the wife of John
Mowry. She was accused of fornication by Comfort
Brewster, a Grand Juror of Lebanon. Brewster states that

around the 7th of April 1795, Thankful, then a single woman known as Thankful Lyman, "did freely permit some man, to your Complaitant unknown, to have & take carnal knowledge of her body & with him did join in carnal copulation, whereby the said Thankful, then a single woman, was impregnated & begotten with Child of a Bastard, which was delivered and born of her body in said Lebanon on the 7th Day of January last, & the said Thankful, ever was a single woman until the birth of said Child." Brewster then names as witnesses, "John Clark, Esquire, and Lucretia Buel, the wife of Capt. Josiah Buel, all of said Lebanon."

• An arrest warrant and report dated 5 August 1796, tells us that William Williams, a County Court Assistant, orders Elisha Hutchinson, a Lebanon Constable, to arrest Thankful Mowry and bring her to Williams' home in Lebanon. The report of the Assistants Court (local Justice Court) reads, in part: "Thankful Mowry, alias Lyman, was by proper officer arrested & brought before this Court by virtue of the foregoing Precept to answer to the foregoing Complaint, & being asked she confessed the facts stated..." Thankful is ordered to appear the third Tuesday in August at the Court of common Pleas of the County of Windham (the County Court).

D. D. Rex vs. Miriam (Wright) Owen, wife of Aaron Owen, of Lebanon; Fornication (before marriage); County Court 25 June 1734; WCCCR, vol. 4. Lebanon vitals note the marriage of Miriam and Aaron without a date. Their daughter Sarah Owen was born 21 May 1733 (LV). Miriam is possibly the daughter of Abel and Rebecca Wright born 14 November 1711 (LV).

D. D. Rex vs. Rachel Paine, of Lebanon; Fornication; County Court June 1749; WCCCR, vol. 12.

D. D. Rex vs. Betty, wife of Jabez Palmer, of Lebanon; Fornication (before marriage); County Court December 1759; WCCCF, box 399. The witness for the time of marriage was Joshua West. Witnesses to the birth on 9 October 1759 were: Widow Elizabeth Clarke and the wife of Lieut. Ezekiel Fitch.

D. D. Rex vs. Lois Ramont(Raymond?) alias Bradford, of Lebanon; Fornication; Writ 18 June 1750; County Court December 1750; WCCCR, vol. 6.

D. D. Rex vs. Joseph & Hannah (Trumble) Sluman/Slewman, of Lebanon; Fornication (before marriage); County Court 22 June 1736; WCCCR, vol. 2. Verdict: Not guilty. The Lebanon vitals state that they were married 27 February 1734/35. Their son Joseph, Jr., was born 2 November 1736. There is a Hannah born to Joseph and Hannah Trumble 18 September 1717 (LV).

D. D. Rex vs. Anne Starkee, wife of Nathan, of Lebanon; Fornication (before marriage) County Court June 1749; WCCCR, vol. 6. Anne did not appear in court.

D. D. Rex vs. Annis/Agnes Sweetland, of Lebanon; Fornication; County Court December 1747; WCCCR, vol. 6. John and Sarah Sweetland had a daughter Agnes born 13 October 1726 (LV). There is a marriage record for Agnes Sweetland and Samuel Brewster, Jr., 30 March 1749 in the Lebanon vitals.

D. D. Rex vs. Ruth (Knowles) Ticknor, wife of Elisha Ticknor, of Lebanon; Fornication (before marriage); County Court 22 June 1757; WCCCF, box 397. The Lebanon vitals tell us that Ruth & Elisha were married 25 November 1756. Their son Elisha was born 25 ----- 1757 (LV). The court files relates that the child was born the "end of March 1757". Elisha (Sr.), is probably the son of John and Mary Ticknor born 26 December 1736 (LV).

Eunice Treat(s), of Lebanon vs. Eleazer Bill. of Lebanon; Maintenance; County Court December 1785; WCCCR, vol. 16. Eleazer Bill, son of Eunice Treats, was born 10 June 1785 "at Dr. Moses Williams' (home)" (LV).

D. D. Rex vs. Silence Tuttle, of Lebanon; Fornication; County Court 23 June 174; WCCCR, vol. 4; Silence could be the daughter of John and Judith Tuttle born 20 December 1723 (LV).

D. D. Rex vs. Hannah West, of Lebanon; Fornication; County Court June 1748; WCCCR, vol. 6. Hannah may be the daughter of John and Deborah West born 13 July 1710 (LV).

D. D. Rex vs. Jerusha (Hinkley) West, of Lebanon; Fornication (before marriage); County Court 22 June 1742; WCCCR, vol. 5. The Lebanon vitals record the marriage of Jerusha Hinkley and Nathan West 20 July 1741. There is a Jerusha, daughter of Nathan and Jerusha West born 21 October 1741 in the Lebanon vitals. Jerusha (Sr.) may be the daughter of Gershom and Mary (Buel) Hinkley born 29 December 1720 (LV).

D. D. Rex vs. Abijah Williams, of Lebanon; Fornication; County Court June 1768; WCCCR, vol. 12.

D. D. Rex vs. Daniel Williams, Jr., and his wife Elizabeth (Twogood), of Lebanon; Fornication (before marriage); County Court 11 December 1733; WCCCR, vol. 2. The marriage is noted without a date in the Lebanon vitals. Jehiel, son of Daniel and Elizabeth Williams, was born 27 May 1732 (LV). (Note: Jehiel died 16 March 1733 (LV).

D. D. Rex vs. Mary Williams, of Lebanon; Fornication; County Court 23 June 1741; WCCCR, vol. 4.

D. D. Rex vs. Grace (Webster) Wise, wife of Samuel Wise, of Lebanon; Fornication (before marriage); County Court June 1751; WCCCR&F, vol. 6 & box 391. Their son Jonathan was born 1 April 1751 (LV), and they were married 3 December 1750 (4 December in Lebanon vitals). Witnesses to the birth were Mrs. Metcalf and the wife of James Bill. Grace is probably the daughter of John and Mary (Dewey) Webster born 29 April 1733 (LV).

Prudence Wise, single woman, of Lebanon vs. Edward Tiffany, of Lebanon; Maintenance; Writ 14 December 1768; County Court June 1769; WCCCR, vol. 6. Prudence's child was born 6 June 1769. Edward may be the son of John and Mary (Meachum) Tiffany born 24 June 1750 (LV).

D. D. Rex vs. Benjamin Wright and his wife Rachel, of Lebanon; Fornication (before marriage); County Court 24 June 1735; WCCCR, vol. 2. Lucy, daughter of Benjamin and Rachel Wright, was born 15 May 1735 (LV).

MANSFIELD, TOLLAND COUNTY, CT

Anne, an Indian, single woman, of Mansfield vs. Samuel Hair, of Mansfield; Maintenance; County Court June 1749; WCCCR, vol. 6. Anne's child, Suse, was born 16 December 1748 (MV). According to the court record Anne was formerly a bound servant to Henry Cleveland of Mansfield. This case was reviewed in December 1749 but the charges and findings remained the same--guilty.

D. D. Rex vs. Patty Baker, single woman, of Mansfield; Fornication; Writ 17 June 1782; County Court December 1782; WCCCR, vol. 15. Patty's child, Luther Eaton, was born 3 June 1782 (MV).

D. D. Rex vs. Dorothy Balch, widow, of Mansfield; Fornication; County Court June 1758; WCCCF, box 398. The court alleged that Dorothy, who had been a widow for more than one year, gave birth to a child on 26 February 1758. Witnesses to the birth were Abigail and Elizabeth Hovey of Mansfield.

D. D. Rex vs. Margaret (Triscott) Balch, wife of John, of Mansfield; Fornication (before marriage); County Court December 1739; WCCCR, vol. 3. Margaret, daughter of Ebenezer Triscott, married John Balch 5 November 1738

(MV). Their daughter Zerviah Balch was born 2 April 1739 (MV).

Dorcas Bassett, single woman, of Mansfield vs. Nathaniel Hunt, of Mansfield; Maintenance; County Court June 1740; WCCCR, vol. 4. Rufus, son of Dorcas, was born 25 January 1739/40 (MV). The case was reviewed again in December. The verdict of "guilty" was upheld plus Nathaniel Hunt had to pay an extra forty shillings (above the usual 6 shillings quarterly to the mother for maintenance of the child) because the child was "very sickly and weakly".

D. D. Rex vs. Hannah Bibbins, single woman, of Mansfield; Fornication; County Court June 1767; WCCCR, vol. 12. Her child Philothea was born 22 December 1766 (MV).

D. D. Rex vs. Mehitable Bosworth, of Mansfield; Fornication; County Court June 1778; WCCCR, vol. 15.

D. D. Rex vs. Sarah (Freeman) Conant, wife of Malachi Conant, of Mansfield; Fornication (before marriage); County Court 2 December 1739; WCCCR, vol. 3. Sarah, the daughter of Edmund Freeman, married Malachi Conant 15 February 1738/39 (MV). Their daughter Lydia Conant was born 26 August 1739 (MV).

Phebe Cross, of Mansfield vs. Isaac Hall, of Mansfield;
Maintenance; Writ 7 January 1782; County Court February
1783; WCCCR, vol.. 16. Phebe's child was born 17 April
1782, in Mansfield.

D. D. Rex vs. Elizabeth Dimmick, of Mansfield; Fornication;
County Court 12 December 1738; WCCCR, vol. 3.

D. D. Rex vs. Phebe Dunham, of Mansfield; Fornication;
County Court June 1769; WCCCR, vol. 12. There is a Phebe,
daughter of Ebenezer, 3rd, and Phebe (Ladd) Dunham, born 28
October 1746.

**D. D. Rex vs. Priscilla (Paddock) Eldridge, wife of Elisha,
of Mansfield;** Fornication (before marriage); County Court 26
June 1744; WCCCR, vol. 5. Married in January 1743, their
daughter Bethiah Eldridge was born 26 February 1743 (MV).

**Violata Fenton, of Mansfield vs. Peter (alias James) Gard-
ner, a transient tailor;** Maintenance; County Court 20 December 1728; WCCCR&F, vol. 1 & box 365. Violata's
daughter was allegedly begotten "last January" (1727/28).
The child, Lucy Harden was born 14 October 1728, in Mansfield (MV). Violata is the daughter of Robert and Dorathe
Fenton born 20 August 1706 (MV).

Anne Fuller, of Mansfield vs. Daniel Fuller, Jr., of Coventry; Maintenance; Writ 26 November 1730; County Court 22 June 1731; WCCCR, vol. 1. Anne, the daughter of Thomas Fuller, of Rehoboth (MA), gave birth to her son David Fuller 22 February 1730/31 (MV). The court record adds, that Anne gave birth "before her marriage." The defendant Daniel Fuller defaulted by not appearing in court and was fined.

D. D. Rex vs. Elizabeth Fuller, of Mansfield; Fornication; County Court June 1767; WCCCR, vol. 12. See Mansfield vitals.

Phebe Ginnings/Jennings, of Mansfield vs. Jonah Case, of Lebanon; Maintenance; County Court December 1774; WCCCR, vol. 14. Phebe's child was born 19 August 1774.

D. D. Rex vs. Susannah (Hatch) Green, wife of Ebenezer, of Mansfield; Fornication (before marriage); County Court 26 June 1739; WCCCR, vol. 3. Susannah is the daughter of John Hatch, deceased, at the time of the trial. She married Ebenezer Green 15 June 1738 and their daughter Sarah was born 5 October 1738 (MV).

D. D. Rex vs. Samuel & Desire (Doty) Jacobs, of Mansfield; Fornication (before marriage); County Court 27 June 1738; WCCCR, vol. 3. Samuel Jacobs, of Mansfield, and Desire Doty, of Windham, were married 11 February

1737/38 and their son Benjamin was born 30 April 1738 (MV). The vitals also state that Desires father was deceased at the time of her marriage.

D. D. Rex vs. Sarah Jacobs, of Mansfield; Fornication; Writ 18 March 1757; WCCCF, box 397. Mansfield residents Mary and Joseph Jacobs, 2nd, and Abigail Anderson were called as witnesses to the birth which took place 25 December 1756 (a boy named "Roger" in the Mansfield vitals). Joseph, Jr., and Mary/Mariah (Storrs) Jacobs had a daughter Sarah born 13 December 1735 (MV).

D. D. Rex vs. Hannah Jaques, of Mansfield; Fornication; County Court December 1766; WCCCR, vol. 11.

D. D. Rex vs. Nathaniel & Ann (Royse) Kidder, of Mansfield; Fornication (before marriage); County Court 26 June 1739 (continued from 27 February 1738/39); WCCCR, vol. 3. Anne, daughter of James Royse, and Nathaniel Kidder were married 15 June 1738 (MV). Nathaniel and Ann's daughter Ann Kidder was born 15 October 1738 (MV).

D. D. Rex vs. Elizabeth King, of Mansfield; Fornication; County Court June 1772; WCCCR, vol. 13.

D. D. Rex vs. Elizabeth Kingsley, of Mansfield; Fornication; County Court June 1769; WCCCR, vol. 12.

D. D. Rex vs. Prudence Leavens, of Mansfield; Fornication; Writ 20 January 1766; County Court June 1766; WCCCR, vol. 11.

D. D. Rex vs. Hannah Porter, single woman, of Mansfield; Fornication; Writ December 1756; WCCCF, box 397. The birth of her daughter Ann on 4 November 1756 (MV), was witnessed by Abigail Easterbrook, Ann Sergeant and Abigail Chance, all of Mansfield.

D. D. Rex vs. Hannah Royse, of Mansfield; Fornication; County Court June 1758; WCCCF, box 398. Hannah's daughter Martha Mercy was born 3 December 1757 (MV). Witnesses were: Desire and Hannah Cross and Abigail Crane, all of Mansfield.

D. D. Rex vs. Jerusha (Hall) Royse, wife of John Royse, of Mansfield; Fornication (before marriage); County Court 12 December 1738; WCCCR, vol. 3. Jerusha, the daughter of Isaac Hall, and John Royse were married 13 April 1738 (MV). Their son John Royse was born 30 June 1738 (MV).

D. D. Rex vs. Miles & Jerusha (Fuller) Standish, of Mansfield; Fornication (before marriage); County Court 27 June 1738; WCCCR, vol. 3. Jerusha, the daughter of Matthew Fuller, married Miles Standish 2 November 1737 (MV). Israel, son of Jerusha and Miles Standish was born 22 April 1738 (MV).

Polly Trumbull, of Mansfield vs. William Campbell, of Mansfield; Maintenance; County Court March 1803; WCCCR, vol. 20. According to the records the child was begotten 23 April 1802 and born 28 December 1802, in Mansfield. The case was appealed in 1803 but the verdict of "guilty" stood.

Mary Walker, of Mansfield vs. Prince Aspinwell, of Mansfield; Maintenance; County Court June 1768; WCCCR, vol. 12. Mary's child, a girl, was born 17 April 1768.

MIDDLETOWN, MIDDLESEX COUNTY, CT

D. D. Rex vs. Mary Wales, now of Middletown, late of Windham; Fornication (before marriage); County Court 27 June 1738; WCCCR, vol. 3

NORWICH, NEW LONDON COUNTY, CT

D. D. Rex vs. Jonathan & Mary Graves, now of Norwich, late of Lebanon; Fornication (before marriage); County Court 27 February 1738/39; WCCCR, vol. 3.

PLAINFIELD, WINDHAM COUNTY, CT

John Barber, for his daughter Betsey, a minor, of Plainfield vs. Nathan Harris, of Plainfield; Maintenance; County Court December 1833; WCCCR, vol. 29. Betsey, a single woman, is "with child" at the time of the trial.

D. D. Rex vs. Elizabeth Fellows, of Plainfield; Fornication; County Court 23 June 1741; WCCCR, vol. 4. Elizabeth may have been the daughter of Isaac and Abigail Fellows born 28 Apr 1722 (PLV).

Town of Plainfield for Mary Ann Fenner vs. Samuel Davis, of Lebanon; Maintenance; County Court 17 December 1828 & March 1829; WCCCR, vol. 29. The court records states that Mary Ann moved with her father's family from Rhode Island to Plainfield a few years before the birth of her child. The child was allegedly begotten 10 March 1828. The case is continued until March. Verdict: Guilty.

Ezekiel Hall for his daughter Betsey, a minor, of Plainfield vs. William Hopkins, of Plainfield; Maintenance; County Court August 1824 & December 1825 & 1826; WCCCR, vol. 28. The child, a female, was begotten 27 July 1823 and born 12 April 1824. The complaint against William Hopkins is withdrawn in 1824 but brought back into court in 1825 with a judgment against Hopkins. The case is heard a third time in 1826 with the Town of Plainfield suing Hopkins for maintenance. The outcome is still a verdict of guilty.

Elizabeth Harris, late of Coventry, now of Plainfield vs. Daniel Edwards, Jr., of Coventry; Maintenance; Writ 1731; WCCCF, box 367.

D. D. Rex vs. Dorothy Harris, alias Wells, of Plainfield; Fornication; County Court 7 December 1732; WCCCR, vol. 2.

D. D. Rex vs. Martha Harris, of Plainfield; Fornication; County Court 10 January 1758; WCCCF, box 398. Martha's child was born 10 January 1758.

Ann Herd, of Plainfield vs. Nathan Harris, Jr., of Plainfield; Maintenance; Writ 27 September 1772; County Court December 1772; WCCCR, vol. 13. Ann's child was allegedly begotten 29 August 1772. Nathan is probably the son of Nathan and Susannah (Rood) Harris, born 8 February 1750 (PLV). Verdict: Not guilty.

Keziah Jordan, of Plainfield vs. Christopher Dean, of Plainfield; Maintenance; Writ 28 September 1770; County Court June 1771; WCCCR, vol. 12.

Nancy Lester, single woman, of Plainfield vs. Daniel Sweet, of Canterbury; Maintenance; County Court December 1827; WCCCR, vol. 28. The male child, begotten 25 December 1826, in Sterling was born 3 September 1827.

Anna Parks, of Plainfield vs. David Gallup, of Plainfield; Maintenance; Writ 24 January 1786; County Court February 1786 & February 1788; WCCCR, vol. 17. The child was born 25 December 1784. Gallup appealed the case twice but the outcome was always the same--guilty. Anna may be the daughter of Nehemiah and Sibbel (Douglass) Parks born 17 August 1760 (PLV). David is probably the son of John and Bridget (Palmer) Gallup born 17 October 1754 (PLV).

D. D. Rex vs. Cristabel Parks, of Plainfield; Fornication ; Writ 27 March 1760; County Court December 1760; WCCCF, box 400. The child was begotten 11 October 1758 and Cristabel swears Robert Parks of Voluntown is the father. There is a marriage record for a Cristabel Parks to Nathaniel Butler 1 October 1761 (PV).

D. D. Rex vs. Advise Sabin, of Plainfield; Fornication; County Court June 1767; WCCCR, vol. 12.

D. D. Rex vs. Susannah Sheppard, of Plainfield; Fornication; County Court 28 June 1743; WCCCR, vol. 5. Susannah is possibly the daughter of Jonas and Mary (Warren) Sheppard born 30 March 1729 (PV).

Martha Welch/Walch, single woman, of Plainfield vs. Joseph Robinson, of Plainfield; Maintenance; County Court 8 December 1730; WCCCR&F, vol. 1 & box 367. Her daughter Elizabeth Robson was born 26 August 1730, and the father named as "Joseph Robson" (PV). Martha may be the daughter of James and Mary Welch born 25 October 1704 (PV).

D. D. Rex vs. Dorothy Wells alias Harris, of Plainfield; Fornication; County Court 7 December 1732; WCCCR, vol. 2.

D. D. Rex vs. Esther Whitney, of Plainfield; Fornication; County Court June 1759; WCCCF, box 399. Esther may be the daughter of David and Elizabeth (Warren) Whitney born 1 May 1714 (PV). Surety for Esther was Ezekiel Whitney.

POMFRET, WINDHAM COUNTY, CT

Mary Adams, late of Oxford, MA, now of Pomfret vs. Stephen Brown II, of Killingly; Maintenance; Writ 14 July 1774; County Court December 1774; WCCCR, vol. 14. Born in Oxford, MA, 15 December 1773, her child died 20 April 1774.

Lois Allen, of Pomfret vs. John Grosvenor, Jr., of Pomfret;
Maintenance; County Court June 1766; WCCCR, vol. 11; The
child was born 23 July 1765. Lois may be the daughter of
David and Mary Allen born 16 April 1745 (POV).

**Joel Baker for his daughter Lucy, a minor, of Pomfret vs.
Samuel Angell, of Pomfret;** Maintenance; County Court
August 1821; WCCCR, vol. 27. Lucy, a single woman, gave
birth to her child on 30 January 1821 in Pomfret. The verdict:
Not guilty.

**Nabby/Abigail Baker, of Pomfret vs. Jesse Russell, of
Brooklyn;** Maintenance; County Court December 1835;
WCCCR, vol. 29; The child is said to have been begotten 15
January 1835, in Hampton, and born 18 August 1835.

**Jemima Cady, of Pomfret vs. Edward Hoystead, of Can-
terbury;** Maintenance; County Court 22 June 1736; WCCCR,
vol. 2. The child was allegedly begotten May 1735. Jemima is
probably the daughter of Ezekiel and Abigail (Cady) Cady born
23 June 1708 (POV).

D. D. Rex vs. Anna Carpenter, a single woman, of Pomfret;
Fornication; County Court June 1769; WCCCR, vol. 12. The
Pomfret vitals record the birth of Lucinda Brewster, Anna's
child, on 27 February 176-. Anna may be the daughter of Si-

mon/Simeon and Sarah (Sawyer) Carpenter born 6 March
1747 (POV).

D. D. Rex vs. Mary Clark, of Pomfret; Fornication; County
Court 22 June 1742; WCCCR, vol. 5.

**Lydia Clement, as of now residing in Pomfret vs. Joseph
Goodell, of Pomfret**; Maintenance; County Court December
1807; WCCCR, vol. 21. Lydia's child was born 16 August
1807.

**D. D. Rex vs. Zerviah Goodale/Goodell, single woman, of
Pomfret**; Fornication; Writ February 1756; WCCCF, box 397.
She gave birth to her child 18 November 1755. Zerviah is the
daughter of Zechariah and Hanna (Cheney) Goodell born 27
February 1730/31 (POV).

D. D. Rex vs. Hannah King, of Pomfret; Fornication; County
Court June 1770; WCCCR, vol. 12.

D. D. Rex vs. Tamar Lee, of Pomfret; Fornication; Writ 16
August 1775; County Court February 1777; WCCCR, vol. 14.

D. D. Rex vs. Abigail Lyon, of Pomfret; Fornication; County
Court February 1775; WCCCR, vol. 14. Abigail could be the

daughter of Jonathan and Elizabeth (Sabin) Lyon born 20 June 1749 (POV).

Abiel Lyon for Experience Lyon, single woman, of Pomfret vs. Edward MacCoy, single man, of Pomfret; Maintenance; Writ 23 January 1726/27; County Court 20 December 1728; WCCCR, vol. 1. The child was begotten August 1726. Abiel Lyon is surety for Experience and James Danielson is surety for Edward MacCoy. Experience Lyon married Ebenezer Goodell 21 October 1728 (POV).

Judith Lyon, of Pomfret vs. Nathaniel Stowell, of Pomfret; Maintenance; Writ 3 May 1732; County Court 1732/33; WCCCR, vol. 2. Judith is probably the daughter of Abiel and Judith Lyon born 5 September 1713 (POV).

D. D. Rex vs. Joanna Sabin, of Pomfret; Fornication; County Court December 1768; WCCCR, vol. 12. Joannah is most likely the daughter of Seth and Joanna (Cady) Sabin born 18 August 1744 (POV).

D. D. Rex vs. Martha Sabin, single woman, of Pomfret; Fornication; Writ 1 August 1749; County Court December 1750; WCCCR, vol. 6. Elihu Cummings, son of Martha Sabin, was born 6 December 1749 (POV). Martha is probably the daughter of Timothy and Martha (Johnson) Sabin born 30 August 1728 (POV).

Mary Spaulding, of Pomfret vs. Isaac Adams, of Pomfret; Maintenance; County Court 13 December 1726; WCCCR, vol. 1.

D. D. Rex vs. Daniel Trowbridge, of Pomfret; Fornication (before marriage); County Court 24 June 1735; WCCCR, vol. 2. Daniel's wife is not named in the suit but there is Daniel Trowbridge and his wife Hannah residing in Pomfret at this time and the births of their children are recorded there.

D. D. Rex vs. Thomas Truesdel & his wife Judith (Leavens), of Pomfret; Fornication (before marriage); County Court 14 December 1736; WCCCR, vol. 3. They were married 20 November 1734 (POV).

D. D. Rex vs. Anna (Grosvenor) Wheeler, wife of Josiah of Pomfret; Fornication (before marriage); County Court 22 June 1736; WCCCR, vol. 2. Anna and Josiah were married 14 December 1735 (POV). Their daughter Mary was born 17 March 1735/36 (POV).

STERLING, WINDHAM COUNTY, CT

Althea Corey, single woman, of Sterling vs. Ira Parkis/Parkhurst; Maintenance; County Court August 1829; WCCCR, vol. 29. Complaint withdrawn.

Sarah Jordan, of Sterling vs. Samuel Cole, of Sterling; Maintenance; County Court March 1804; WCCCR, vol. 20.

THOMPSON, WINDHAM COUNTY, CT

Robe Arnold, single woman, of Thompson vs. Riel Converse, of Thompson; Maintenance; Writ 9 February 1802; County Court August 1802; WCCCR&F, vol. 20 & box 433. Robe's child was born 13 March 1802, in Thompson. Riel is probably the son of Elijah & Experience Converse born 24 February 1782 (KV). Among the documents in File box 433:

- Complaint of Robe Arnold, single woman, of Thompson. She states that on 14 June 1801 Riel Converse, "did beget her with child..." Robe asks that he be arrested and ordered to pay maintenance and support for the child when it is born. Dated 9 February 1802.

    The second part of the instrument is an order to Amos Cummins of Thompson to arrest Riel Converse and have him brought before Jason Phipps, Justice of the Peace, at the home of Daniel Arnold in Thompson to answer the charges made by Robe Arnold. This is also dated 9 February 1802. The fee paid by Daniel Arnold was $40 for "prosecution according to Law" plus a .34 duty (tax).

- Amos Cummins in his report states that he has arrested Riel Converse and has brought him to Daniel Arnold's house to appear before Jason Phipps, Justice of the Peace. Dated 9 February 1802.

- A Justice Court is held at Daniel Arnold's house in Thompson. The parties both request that the case be adjourned to 13 April 1802. Elijah Converse and Daniel Bennett agree to act as surety for Converse and Arnold. The child has been born alive so the complaint continues. Riel Converse is ordered to appear before the County Court in Windham on the third Tuesday of August 1802.

- There are summons for Jason Phipps, Timothy Somes, Chester Upham, Oliver ------, Smith Arnold, and Lucy Arnold. These are signed by Jason Phipps, John Stone, and John McClellan all dated August 1802.

- The file record of the County Court proceedings tells us that Robe's child was born 13 March 1802, "and the same is now alive and stands in need of support and maintenance." The defendant's plea is recorded as "not guilty". The reverse side of the proceedings lists all the expenses incurred by the case ($34.34 court costs) and the verdict of "guilty". Just below "Robe Arnold vs. Riel Converse" are the terms set for his payments for support and maintenance. A torn piece of missing page seems to outline the court's decision with the particular terms of support stipulated. It suggests that Riel Converse will have to support the child for a total of four years and also pay "the costs of the girl's lying in."

Elizabeth Robbins, of Thompson vs. Joseph Sheffield, of Dudley, MA; Maintenance; Writ 13 May 1791; County Court December 1791; WCCCR&F, vol. 18 & box 422. Elizabeth's child was born 10 April 1791, in Thompson. There are three marriages for Joseph Sheffield in the Dudley, MA, vitals. Among the documents were the following:

- A copy of the Complaint addressed, "to Jason Phipps, Esq., Justice of the Peace for Windham County in the State of Connecticut -- Elizabeth Robbins, of Thompson, upon a certain statute of law of this State Intitled an Act concerning (page torn) & Bastardy, complaint makes ---------- Information --------Day of April last past she was delivered of a Bastard Child of her body Begotten on or about the Tenth Day of July 179-- by Joseph Sheffield of Dudley in the County of Worcester in the Commonwealth of Massachusetts that the now said Joseph Sheffield is the f(a)ther of said --- child, and that said Bastard Child is now alive ---------- want support and maintenance and said Joseph Sheffield neglect --- and refuses to provide for or support -----..." Dated 13 May 17-- and signed with Elizabeth Robbins' mark. Elizabeth Robbins appeared before Jason Phipps, was "duly examined" and swore as to the veracity of her statement.

- The next document is an arrest warrant for Joseph Sheffield. Sheffield is ordered to go before Jason Phipps to answer the Complaint of Elizabeth Robbins. The defendant's plea of is "not guilty". The second side of the warrant is a list of expenses dated September 1791. It is signed by Jason Phipps, Justice of the Peace.

- A constable for the Town of Thompson, (page torn) Russell, reports that he has arrested Joseph Sheffield who will then appear before Jason Phipps, Justice of the Peace. Russell notes his fees for this service. Under the title "Pleadings" Sheffield alleges his innocence and that he will represent himself.

  In the last paragraph, dated 5 September 1791, it is reported that a hearing was held before Jason Phipps on the Complaint of Elizabeth Robbins against Joseph Sheffield. The court finds him guilty and he is bound "with sufficient surety" to appear before the Court of Common Pleas, "to be holden at Windham in and for the County of Win(dham) (Page torn).

- The Deposition of Lucy Webster: "I Lucy Webster of Thompson in Windham County testify and say that on the tenth day of April last I was called in to the house where Elizabeth Robbins then was and when I came into the house to my great astonishment found a number of women there; and the said Elizabeth in distress. I was called on to officiate as a midwife for her and I found her to be with child and in travil, I then asked her in the most serious and solemn manner I could to tell me whose child it was that she was then in travil with. Elizabeth answered she had as leaves tell me as not and then said it was Joseph Sheffield's child and nobodies else, and it was ------ to wave the delivery until somebody could be had to further examine said Elizabeth and Capt. Peleg Corbin came in just before the child was born and examined her and she told him likewise that Joseph Sheffield was the father of the c(hild). One of the women asked if Joseph Sheffield would force women; it was answered by a woman present he will nearly force them against their will, and since said Elizabeth was delivered of the child aforesaid she told your deponent that Joseph Sheffield had worried her to force her before the time when he begat her with child. And your deponent further saith not. Thompson, December 13th, 1791. Signed Lucy Webster, with her mark.

Question asked by the Justice: What is Elizabeth Robbins character as to truth. Answer by the deponent: I have reason to believe she told me the truth."

- The deposition of Peleg Corbin. "I Peleg Corbin of Thompson in Windham County testify and say that on the tenth day of April last I was requested by one of the neighbors of Elisabeth Robbins in said Thompson to examine the said Elisabeth concerning the bastard child with which she was then in travail and accordingly your deponent went to the house where said Elisabeth was; and she was then in her distress. I then asked her in a solemn manner who was the father of the child she was then pregnant with and she, the said Elisabeth, answered without hesitation that Joseph Sheffield was the father and no other and the said Elisabeth was delivered of the said child in about four or five minutes afterward. And your deponent further saith not. Thompson, December the 12th, 1791. Signed Peleg Corbin."

- The Deposition of Thomas Holbrook and his wife Abigail, of Thompson.(This document was torn and in poor condition.) They attest to the honesty and upright character of Elizabeth Robbins, who now lives with them. They trust her enough to give her, "the Keys of our House, Desk, Chests, & whatever..." Both signed the document which is dated 17 December 1791.

- The next deposition is that of John Whitmore, Jr., of Thompson (document in very poor condition). He also testifies as to the honesty of Elizabeth Robbins. Signed and dated 17 December 1791.

- Deposition of Betsey Healy, wife of Ezra Healy of Thompson. She testifies that on 7 December 1791 Reuben Chamberlain and his wife were visiting at her home. Mrs. Chamberlain asked Mother Holbrook how long Elizabeth Robbins was going to live with her. "Mama told her that she intended to keep her as long as she could for she said they like her. Mrs. Chamberlain answered my mother she hoped she would. Tho, it was a great trouble to keep a young child in the house, for Mrs. Chamberlain said she counted Elizabeth was a Clever girl, and was called so when she lived in Charlton. Mrs. Chamberlain said she knew her all the while she lived in Charlton and your deponent further saith not." Betty Healy left her mark on the document dated 17 December 1791.

- On the same form was the deposition of Abigail Whitemore, wife of John, of Thompson. She also attests to Elizabeth's honesty. Marked and dated 17 December 1791.

- John Bowers, Jr., of Thompson testifies that he and Joseph Sheffield visited the house of John Robbins the evening after the birth of Elizabeth's child. John says that he heard Elizabeth accuse Joseph Sheffield of being the father of her child. Several other people, including Sheffield, questioned Elizabeth and she answered them all the same. John Bowers, Jr., signed the paper dated 12 December 1791.

- Mary, the wife of Joshua Robbins, of Dudley, testifies under oath that she was present at John Robbins' house in Thompson when Elizabeth Robbins was in labor with her child. She heard Elizabeth declare that Joseph Sheffield was the father of her child. This took place the beginning of April 1791. Mary signed with her "x". Dated 12 December 1791.

- Molly Coburn, the wife of Jonathan of Thompson testifies that Elizabeth Robbins was hired by them for some time the year before for what seems to be several months or more. Molly states that Elizabeth is truthful. Signed and dated 17 December 1791.

- Both Rufus Brown and John Whitmore of Thompson certify that Nathan Brown has the means to "answer all costs" in Elizabeth Robbins' case. Signed and dated 16 December 1791. Nathan Brown had been certified by Jason Phipps to act as bondsman for Elizabeth Robbins.
- A document concerning the forfeiture of bonds by Darius Bacon, attorney for Joseph Sheffield.
- There is also a writ that is an attempt by Joseph Sheffield to ask the court to "abate & dismiss" the charges against him.

A statement made by Elizabeth Robbins at the Windham County County Court proceedings in December 1791. She testifies that the child she bore was begotten on her body by Joseph Sheffield and that the child was born in Windham County. Both these details were omitted from the original complaint say Sheffield's lawyers and may have been the points of contention used by them to plea Joseph Sheffield as "innocent".

UNION, TOLLAND COUNTY, CT

D. D. Rex vs. Mary Salmon, of Union; Fornication; County Court June 1772; WCCCR, vol. 13. Mary is probably the daughter of Sarah Paull born 3 December 1758 (UV).

VOLUNTOWN, WINDHAM COUNTY, CT

Mary Adams, of Voluntown vs. John Anderson, son of John, of Killingly; Maintenance; County Court 15 February 1750/51; WCCCF, box 392. The child, Mary says, was begotten the 26th or 27th December 1750, "in her father's chamber", in Voluntown.

Martha Brown, of Voluntown vs. Edward Robinson, of Westerly, RI; Maintenance; Writ 8 January 1736 ; County Court 14 December 1736; WCCCR, vol. 3. No one appeared in court; her (unnamed) surety must pay the court costs.

Elizabeth Cile (Jr.), of Voluntown vs. John Dixon, of Voluntown; Maintenance; County Court June 1750; WCCCR, vol. 6 Elizabeth's daughter was born 24 November 1749.

Mary Cole, of Voluntown vs. Benadam Gallup, of Voluntown; Maintenance; County Court June 1783; WCCCR, vol. 16. The birth of Elizabeth, daughter of Mary Cole, is recorded in the Voluntown vitals as 21 February 1783, reputed father Benadam Gallup. Benadam may be the son of Isaac and Margaret (Gallup) Gallup born 17 November 1761, who married Elizabeth Dorrance 31 March 1785   (VV).

D. D. Rex vs. Elizabeth Fair/Fare, of Voluntown; Fornication; County Court December 1774; WCCCR, vol. 14.

D. D. Rex vs. Grace Fair/Fare, of Voluntown; Fornication; County Court December 1774; WCCCR, vol. 14. Grace is probably the daughter of John & Hannah Fair born 31 May 1751 (VV).

D. D. Rex vs. Mehitable Jeffords, single woman of Voluntown; Fornication; County Court 22 January 1750/51; WCCCF, box 391. According to the files Mehitable's child was born about 23 September 1750 at Joshua Jefford's house. The witnesses were: Hannah Cogswell, midwife, and wife of Edward Cogswell, of Preston; Mary, wife of James Kinne; Abigail, wife of Moses Kinne; Elizabeth Crery; and Sarah Springer, all of Voluntown. Mehitable is probably the daughter of Joshua and Ann Jeffords born 10 July 1720 (VV).

Martha Parke, single woman, of Voluntown vs. John Smith, Jr., of Voluntown; Maintenance; Writ 23 March 1759; County Court December 1759; WCCCF, box 399. Martha could be the daughter of Robert and Dorothy (Bacon) Parke born 21 July 1725 (VV). John is probably the son of John and Phebe (Pierce) Smith born 4 September 1737 (VV).

Sarah Plympton, single woman, late of Plainfield, now of Voluntown vs. Edmon Jordan/Gordon, of Voluntown;

Charge Maintenance; Writ 3 August 1728; County Court 24 June 1729; WCCCR&F, vol. 1 & box 366. According to the court record and files Sarah's child was begotten last June at Widow Gurdon's in Voluntown. Testimony tells us, "She has not had any other." The date of birth is not given but in a list of charges she presents, Sarah lists as expenses: Midwife, sugar, rum, victuals, and clothes (list not dated). Witnesses: John Smith and Samuel Church, of Voluntown. Edmon cannot pay so he is bound out to his surety, John Dixon. Stephen Gurdon is also listed as surety for Edmon on one document.

D. D. Rex vs. Obadiah Rhodes & his wife Abigail, of Voluntown; Fornication (before marriage); County Court 26 June 1733; WCCCR, vol. 2. See Voluntown vitals.

Elizabeth Roth, single woman, of Voluntown vs. William Borman/Boardman, of Voluntown; Fornication; Writ 7 February 1757; County Court June 1757; WCCCF, box 397. The child, male, was begotten the beginning of May 1756 and born 6 February 1757. Documents found in the file included the following:

- First is a copy of Elizabeth Roth's complaint against William Borman stating that he is the father of her child which was delivered the sixth of February. Elizabeth signed with her mark. On the same document is the arrest warrant for William Borman signed by John Smith, Justice of the Peace. Next, the report of Robert Samson, Sheriff's Deputy, stating that he has brought William Borman to the house of Hugh Kennedy for questioning by John Crary,

Justice of the Peace. These documents are all signed 7
February 1757.

- Second, Justice of the Peace, Jeremiah Kinne of Voluntown, states that Elizabeth Roth, single woman, of Voluntown has brought him the complaint against William
Borman, also of Voluntown. Kinne states that she swears
Borman is the father of her child and this occurred about
the first of May at the house of Charles Campbell, Voluntown. Borman, a single man, she says, promised to marry
her. Since that time William Borman, has joined the army.
Signed by Jeremiah Kinne 22 December 1756.

- A record of the small claims court held in Voluntown
on 7 February 1757 stating that the case of Roth vs. Borman will be heard at the June session of the Windham
County County Court.

- A record of the arrest of William Borman 7 July 1757
by Nathaniel Wales, Jr., Sheriff of Windham County

- Summons for Hugh Kennedy, John Cambell, Jr., and
Jeannet Brown, all of Voluntown, to appear before Robert
Dixon, Justice of the Peace, at Lieut. Charles Campbell's
home in said Voluntown, at 3 p.m. on the 27 June 1757.
They are to "give evidence" in the case of Elizabeth Roth
vs. William Borman. Signed Robert Dixon and given to
Noah Briggs, an indifferent (impartial) person to serve no-
tice.

- The Deposition of Hugh Kennedy of Voluntown. He
swears he heard Elizabeth Roth say that William Borman
was the father of her child. Elizabeth was at his home to
deliver her child and stayed with them five weeks and then
went to Mr. Brown's house. During this time she still insisted that William Borman was the father of her child.
Signed Hugh Kennedy and Robert Dixon, Justice of the
Peace, 27 June 1757.

•   Next, the "Deposition of Jeannet Brown of Voluntown in Windham County testifies and saith that, some of January last past she was at the house of John Campbell, Jr., of said Voluntown the next day after William Borman came from the army and Elizabeth Roth was then there, I wished her much joy and asked her if she was not glad her man was come home. She made answer she was sorry for Borman and said that if she had not been persuaded and in a manner fast or she never would have sworn her child upon Borman and she also said that she hold up her covenant hand but did not swear it upon him, and further tho says that she was at the house of Hugh Kennedy on the fourth & fifth days of February last past and also in the morning of the sixth day of said February before day when said Elizabeth was in travail and delivered of a bastard child begotten of her body, and in that time she heard Margaret Trumball of said town who then served as a midwife to deliver said Elizabeth, examine her several times concerning who was the father of her child and said Elizabeth constantly said that said William Borman and no other was the father of her said child, and the Deponent further saith that on the second Tuesday of March last said Elizabeth came to my house, to work some time in ye latter end of said March I understood my Brother Samuel Stewart had given her Encouragement that he would assist her in her case against Borman for the support of her child and manage her said case for her, and further says that some time in the first part of May last, she heard said Stewart tell said Elizabeth that her case was so scandalous a case and that she was such a devilish liar that he believed her case would go against her, and did not care to have any co----with it, and also told her that John Campbell, Jr.'s wife would witness against her that she told her, Charles Campbell, Jr., had to do with her in March and sundry

other times and then she told him that John Campbell's
wife would never say that, she told her that it was said
Charles Campbell, and after said Stewart was gone the
Deponent further says that said Elizabeth told her that ,
that what Stewart had said was true for she had told said
John Campbell's wife so, and I asked her why she accused
said Borman when he was innocent, she said that (she) had
reason to accuse him, said Borman, for he had to do with
her in Lieut. Campbell's chamber, and further says that said
Elizabeth said she intended to clear Said Borman and,
further says that in the latter end of may last, or the beginning of June instant, I heard her desire said Stewart to
tell Borman to come to her, and he told her he would en-
deavor to let Borman know, and the next day in the forenoon William Borman, John Campbell. Jr., and Mr. William
Trumball came to the house of the deponent, as she saith,
and also that at the same time Mr. Trumball told them he
was in hurry to go home and if they had anything to say to
him to let him hear it and then said John Campbell said to
Elizabeth that he understood that she was about to clear
Borman and also that her grandfather was there and he
would give her good advise, and then Mr. Trumball gave
her advise and cautioned her against false swearing and the
danger of lying and she said she did not intend to go to
court nor that Borman should pay any thing for the
maintenance of her child, and then said Borman,
Defendant, spoke with her in private, they viz. she and said
Borman went out together and after a little time came in
again and she said that she cleared Borman for that he was
not the father of her child, and asked his forgiveness.
Signed Jeannet Brown.

A question asked at the Deponent, whether the said
John Campbell did not desire her to see if said Elizabeth

would own before her husband and her, that Borman was not the father of her child. Answer yes.

Question asked at the deponent whether said John
Campbell did not tell said Elizabeth that he would rather give her fifty pounds out of his own pocket that should undo her own soul for fear of the want of money or words to that purpose. Answer yes.
Windham, Voluntown, June the 27th day, A.D., 1757, then personally appeared Jeannet Brown the above Deponent and made solemn oath to the truth of the above within written deposition. The Deponent living more than twenty miles from the State House in Windham, and the aforesaid party being notified and present before me. Signed, Robert Dixon, Justice of the Peace."

- A summons to Margaret Trumbell, Rachel Kennedy, Mariam Kennedy, and Jeannet Campbell, all of Voluntown, to appear at the house of Charles Campbell, Voluntown, at 9 a.m. on the 3rd Tuesday in June to give testimony in the case of Elizabeth Roth vs. William Borman. Signed by John Smith, Justice of the Peace.

- Deposition of Margaret Trumbull of Voluntown who was called to Hugh Kennedy's house 4 February 1757 to act as midwife for Elizabeth Roth who was "in traval". Several times during the weekend Margaret questioned Elizabeth as to the paternity of her child. Even when, "it appeared very likely that she should die", Elizabeth insisted the father was William Borman. Rachel Kennedy was also present at some time and heard Elizabeth's answer. A male child was born on Sunday, 6 February. Signed with her mark Margaret Trumbull and Robert Dixon, Justice of the Peace, 27 June 1757.

- The Deposition of Jeannet Campbell: "Jeannet Campbell of Voluntown in Windham County being of lawful age do testify and say that some time in the Spring of the year 1756, and according to the best of my remembrance, it was some time in May, Elizabeth Roth came to my house and asked me for a pair of loom cards. William Borman of said town being then a weaving in the Chamber in my house, and I then told her to go up into the chamber to him and get them accordingly she went up into the Chamber where he was, and I thought no more about her for some considerable time, but only that she was gone home, but some time after I saw her come down out of the Chamber and went out at the fore door, and I then wondered why she had stayed so long in the Chamber with him but she went out and went away, without saying anything, and I thought no more about it till after I heard that said Elizabeth was with child and that she said that said Borman was the father of her child and then I remembered her going up into the Chamber and staying with Bormans above expressed and which caused me then to think much about he so long staying in ye Chamber at said time. Jeannet Campbell, her mark.

Question being asked the Deponent by said Borman if it was in the day time when said Elizabeth went up into the Chamber and what time of ye day. Answer it was in the day time and according to the best of her remembrance it was in the forenoon.

Windham, Voluntown, June the 28th day, A.D., 1757, then personally appeared Jeannet Cambell, the above Deponent and made solemn oath to the truth of the above written Deposition, the Deponent living more than twenty miles from the State house in Windham, and the adverse party being notified and present before me. Signed Robert Dixon, Justice of the Peace"

- Statement certifying that Lieut. George Crary enlisted William Borman in the army 14 April 1756. Signed Lieut. Thomas Gallup.
- A directive to the Sheriff from Samuel Gray, Treasurer of the Windham County Court. Elizabeth has won her case but has yet to receive payment from William Borman. The sheriff is to find Borman, recover the maintenance and support owed . "You are hereby Commanded to Take the Body of the said William Borman and Commit unto the Keeper of the Gaol in Windham in the County aforesaid, the said prison...until he Pay unto said Elizabeth Roth the full Sums..." Dated 1 July 1757 and signed by Samuel Gray.

D. D. Rex vs. Abigail Springer, single woman, of Voluntown; Fornication; County Court 11 December 1733; WCCCR, vol. 2. Surety for Abigail was James Springer, of Voluntown.

D. D. Rex vs. Patience Stewart, of Voluntown; Fornication; County Court June 1770; WCCCR, vol. 12.

Town of Voluntown for Hannah Weaver, single woman, a pauper, of Voluntown vs. Ebenezer Huntington, of Windham; Maintenance; County Court December 1810; WCCCR, vol. 23. Hannah's child was born 9 August 1810, in Windham. The case was appealed March 1811 but the guilty verdict held. The Windham vitals record the marriage of an Ebenezer Huntington and Lydia Peck of Franklin 10 September 1810. See the next case.

Town of Voluntown for Hannah Weaver, single woman, a pauper, of Voluntown vs. Town of Windham; Maintenance; County Court December 1816 & 6 August 1819; WCCCR, vol. 26. The birth date of this child is not given but the child is living. Hannah and her child are poor and relying on the Town of Voluntown for support. Mason Huntington, of Windham, is allegedly the father. He was arrested but then escaped from jail and "gone to parts unknown". The suit is brought by the town for the recovery of costs of maintaining the child and Hannah. Hannah may have married William Billings of North Stonington 18 August 1822 (VV). Mason could be the son of Daniel and Martha Huntington born 11 February 1792; married Sally Parsons 19 March 1819 (WV).

WILLINGTON, TOLLAND COUNTY, CT

D. D. Rex vs. Mary, wife of Ebenezer Dimmick, of Willington; Fornication (before marriage); County Court 9 December 1740; WCCCR, vol. 4.

WINDHAM, WINDHAM COUNTY, CT

D. D. Rex vs. Eunice Abbe, of Windham; Fornication; County Court December 1774; WCCCR, vol. 14. Eunice, most likely the daughter of Isaac and Eunice (Church) Abbe, was born 12 April 1755; married Jonah Linkon 21 November 1775 (WV).

D. D. Rex vs. Zerviah Abbe, of Windham; Fornication; County Court June 1779; WCCCR, vol. 15. See Windham vitals.

D. D. Rex vs. Freelove (Burgess) Abbot, wife of Stephen, of Windham; Fornication (before marriage); Writ 12 May 1750; County Court 3 June 1751; WCCCR, vol. 6. Freelove and Stephen were married 3 January 1749/50 (WV). Their son was born 21 March 1750.

Mehitable Allen, of Windham vs. Benjamin Brown, of Windham; Maintenance; Writ 5 November 1783; County Court December 1784; WCCCR, vol. 16. The child was born 5 March 1784. Mehitable may be the daughter of Joseph Allen, Jr. & his wife Rebeckah (Robinson), born 15 March 1765 (WV).

D. D. Rex vs. Mary Bass, single woman, of Windham; Fornication; Writ August 1756; WCCCF, box 397. A male child was born to Mary on 21 May 1756. Witnesses to the birth were Prudence, wife of Nathaniel Wales; Elizabeth, wife of Henry Bass; and Widow Sarah Spencer, all of Windham. Mary may be the daughter of Thomas and Dorothy (Parish) Bass born 20 June 1729 (WV).

D. D. Rex vs. Martha (Baker) Bingham, wife of Nathaniel, of Windham; Fornication (before marriage); County Court June 1758; WCCCF, box 398. Martha and Nathaniel were married 2 January 1757 (WV). Their child, a boy, was born 11 June 1757.

D. D. Rex vs. Eunice Burnham, of Windham; Fornication; County Court June 1748; WCCCR, vol. 6.

D. D. Rex vs. Elizabeth Cary, of Windham; Fornication; County Court June 1747; WCCCR, vol. 6.

D. D. Rex vs. Mehitable Cary, of Windham; Fornication; County Court December 1766; WCCCR, vol. 11.

Prudence Champlin, of Windham vs. Gurdon Hebard, of Windham; Maintenance; County Court March 1824; WCCCR, vol. 28. The child, a male, was begotten on 22 November 1822 and born 22 August 1823, in Windham. Prudence may have married Lester Webster of Rochester, NY, 24 January 1830 (WV).

D. D. Rex vs. Eunice (Webb) Cook, wife of Samuel, of Windham; Fornication (before marriage); County Court 10 October 1751; WCCCF, box 391. Samuel and Eunice were married 31 March 1751 (WV); their daughter Sybell Cook was born 3 September 1751 (WV).

D. D. Rex vs. Hannah (Masoloy/Mosely) Curtis, wife of John, Jr., of Windham; Fornication (before marriage); Writ May 1752; WCCCF, box 395. Hannah and John were married 1 May 1753. Their daughter Abigail Curtis was born 17 November 1753, and the court files also mention the time--4 a.m.

Patience Dean, of Windham vs. Judah Back, of Windham; Maintenance; County Court December 1798; WCCCR, vol. 19. Patience's child was born 22 Oct 1798, in Windham. Verdict: Not guilty.

D. D. Rex vs. Elizabeth Dennison, of Windham; Fornication; County Court June 1745; WCCCR, vol. 6.

D. D. Rex vs. Eunice Downer, of Windham; Fornication; County Court 22 June 1742; WCCCR, vol. 5. Eunice's son Jonathan Carver was born 18 December 1741 (WV). The reputed father said to be Jonathan Carver.

D. D. Rex vs. Lois (Moulton) Durgee; Fornication (before marriage); County Court 23 February 1730/31; WCCCR, vol.

1. Verdict: Not guilty. Stephen Durkee married Lois Moulton 19 March 1729/30; their daughter Lois was not born until 1739/40. (Source: Bernice B. Gunderson, a Durkee descendant.)

D. D. Rex vs. Sarah (Durkee) Durkee, wife of Robert, of Windham; Fornication (before marriage); County Court 17 May 1755; WCCCF, vol. box 397. Sarah and Robert were married 21 November 1754 (WV). Their daughter Sarah Durkee was born 5 March 1755 in the Windham vitals--the files say twins were born on that date.

D. D. Rex vs. Elizabeth (Fitch) Durkee, wife of John, of Windham; Fornication (before marriage) ; County Court September 1754; WCCCF, box 395. A daughter was born 13 September 1753.

Mary Ellis/Elice, of Windham vs. James Flint, of Windham; Maintenance; Writ 7 November 1744; County Court December 1744; WCCCR, vol. 6. She is "with child" as of writ. The case is continued until June 1745 but there is no further record of this case. Mary may have married David Read 28 December 1746 (WV).

D. D. Rex vs. Manasseh & Keziah (Ford) Farnham, of Windham; Fornication (before marriage); County Court December 1739; WCCCR, vol. 3. Manasseh and Keziah were married 23 April 1739; their son Manasseh Farnham was born 29 July 1739 (WV).

D. D. Rex vs. Elizabeth (Scott) Fisk, wife of Jonathan, of Windham; Fornication (before marriage); County Court December 1750; WCCCR, vol. 6. Elizabeth and Jonathan were married 9 August 1750 (WV); son John was born 18 December 1750 (WV).

D. D. Rex vs. Sarah Flint, of Windham; Fornication; County Court 28 June 1743; WCCCR, vol. 5.

Lydia Frame, of Windham vs. Samuel Webb, of Windham; Maintenance; County Court 28 June 1743; WCCCR, vol. 5. Nathaniel Webb was surety for Samuel Webb. Lydia may have married William Shaw, Jr., 15 October 1749 (WV).

D. D. Rex vs. Henry Gibson & his wife Hannah, of Windham; Fornication (before marriage); County Court 28 June 1741; WCCCR, vol. 4.

D. D. Rex vs. Joseph Ginnings/Jennings, Jr., & his wife Sarah (Hovey), of Windham; Fornication (before marriage); County Court 9 December 1735; WCCCR, vol. 2. They were married 15 April 1735 in Windham (WV). See Windham vitals.

D. D. Rex vs. Maryah Ginnings/Jennings, of Windham;
Fornication; County Court June 1748; WCCCR, vol. 6.

D. D. Rex vs. Abigail Hammond, of Windham; Fornication;
County Court June 1750; WCCCR, vol. 6.

D. D. Rex vs. Elizabeth (Pearl) Hibbard, of Windham;
Fornication (before marriage); County Court June 1749;
WCCCR, vol. 6.

**D. D. Rex vs. John Hibbard & his wife Martha (Durkee)
Hibbard, of Windham;** Fornication (before marriage);
County Court 1726; WCCCR, vol. 1. John and Martha were
married 22 September 1725 (WV). Martha, the daughter of
John and Martha Hibbard, was born 21 December 1725 (WV).
John may be the son of Robert and Mary Hibbard born 30
October 1704 (WV). There is a Martha Durkee born to Wil-
liam and Rebecka 11 December 1705 (WV).

D. D. Rex vs. Sibbel Hibbard, of Windham; Fornication;
County Court June 1772; WCCCR, vol. 13. See the Windham
vitals.

**D. D. Rex vs. Sarah (Flint), wife of Zebediah Holt, of
Windham;** Fornication (before marriage); County Court 12

December 1732; WCCCR, vol. 2. They were married 14
August 1732; their daughter Eunice was born 8 October 1732
(WV).

D. D. Rex vs. Bethia Howard, single woman, of Windham;
Fornication; County Court 13 December 1756; WCCCF, box
397. Bethiah's child, a boy, was born 1 April 1755.

D. D. Rex vs. Judah Hudson, of Windham; Fornication;
County Court 23 June 1741; WCCCR, vol. 4.

**D. D. Rex vs. James Keyes/Kyes & his wife Tabitha, of
Windham;** Fornication (before marriage); County Court June
1746; WCCCR, vol. 6.

D. D. Rex vs. Sarah Kingsbury, of Windham; Fornication;
County Court June 1750; WCCCR, vol. 6.

D. D. Rex vs. Lydia Kingsley, of Windham; Fornication;
County Court 28 February 1743/44; WCCCR, vol. 5. Lydia
may be the daughter of John and Elizabeth (Bass) Kingsley
born 20 July 1717 (WV).

D. D. Rex vs. Cloa Laidly, of Windham; Fornication; County
Court December 1749; WCCCR, vol. 6.

D. D. Rex vs. Jael Lilly, of Windham; Fornication; County Court June 1769; WCCCR, vol. 12. See Windham vitals "Joel Lilly".

D. D. Rex vs. Mary, wife of Richard Lilly, of Windham; Fornication (before marriage); County Court 12 December 1732; WCCCR, vol. 2.

D. D. Rex vs. Sarah Loomis, of Windham; Fornication; County Court June 1770; WCCCR, vol. 12. Sarah may be the daughter of John and Mary (Fuller) Loomis born 14 April 1751 who married Henry Durkee, Jr., 23 April 1778 (WV).

Mercy Luce, of Windham vs. Ephraim McGuithy, of Preston; Maintenance; Writ 5 December 1740; County Court 9 December 1740; WCCCR, vol. 4. The child was born before the court date but the exact date was not given.

D. D. Rex vs. Phebe Manning, of Windham; Fornication; County Court June 1746; WCCCR, vol. 6.

D. D. Rex vs. Zerviah Norwood, of Windham; Fornication; Writ 18 December 1764; County Court December 1764; WCCCR, vol. 11. Zerviah's son, Jonathan Arms, was born 20 October 1764 (WV). Zerviah may have married James Dailey 19 August 1766 (WV).

D. D. Rex vs. Hannah Palmer, of Windham; Fornication; County Court June 1767; WCCCR, vol. 12.

D. D. Rex vs. Dorothy Parish, of Windham; Fornication; County Court December 1749; WCCCR, vol. 6.

D. D. Rex vs. Elizabeth (Bourn) Philips, wife of John, of Windham; Fornication (before marriage); County Court 12 December 1738; WCCCR, vol. 3. John and Elizabeth were married 2 February 1737/38 (WV). Their daughter Sarah Philips was born 18 June 1738 (WV).

D. D. Rex vs. Joseph Preston, 2nd, & his wife Mary (Frame) Preston, of Windham; Fornication (before marriage); County Court 27 June 1738; WCCCR, vol. 3. According to the Windham vitals Joseph and Mary were married 8 April 1738 (WV).

Martha Preston, of Windham vs. Dr. Jeremiah Selva, now deceased, late of New Haven; Maintenance; County Court 17 May 1727; WCCCR&F, vol. 1 & box 364. According to the court records the child was begotten April 1726 and born January 1727. Daniel Dutton, administrator of Dr. Selva's estate must answer the charges.

D. D. Rex vs. Martha Preston, of Windham; Fornication; County Court June 1772; WCCCR, vol. 13.

Jerusa Ripley, of Windham vs. Elias Frink, of Windham; Maintenance; Writ 4 May 1731; County Court 1731-1732; WCCCR, vol. 2. In 1732 Jerusa withdraws the complaint but Elias is still held responsible by the court and must pay for the child's maintenance. Jerusa is probably the daughter of Joshua and Hannah (Bradford) Ripley born 1 November 1704 (WV).

D. D. Rex vs. Hannah Robbins, of Windham; Fornication; County Court December 1744; WCCCR, vol. 6.

D. D. Rex vs. Rebekah Robbins, of Windham; Fornication; County Court June 1748; WCCCR, vol. 6.

D. D. Rex vs. Hannah Rogers, of Windham; Fornication; County Court June 1748; WCCCR, vol. 6.

D. D. Rex vs. Mary (Wedge) Rounding/Roundy, of Windham; Fornication (before marriage); Writ 11 September 1770; County Court June 1771; WCCCR, vol. 12.

D. D. Rex vs. Robert Rounding/Roundy & his wife Elizabeth (Green), of Windham; Fornication (before marriage); County Court 13 December 1726; WCCCR&F, vol. 1 & box 363. Robert and Elizabeth were married 15 February 1725/26 (WV); their son John Rounding/Roundy was born 23 August 1726 (WV).

D. D. Rex vs. Ann Rudd, single woman, of Windham; Fornication; Writ June 1752; WCCCF, box 392. The birth of Ann's daughter took place on 10 April 1752. Witnesses to the birth were: Prudence, wife of Nathan Wales; Rachel, wife of Joseph Bingham; and Sarah, wife of Joseph Bingham, Jr. All the witnesses reside in Windham.

D. D. Rex vs. Elizabeth Shaw, single woman, of Windham; Fornication; Writ 20 May 1731; County Court 22 June 1731; WCCCR, vol. 1. On the 8th or 9th of April, 1731, in the house of Ebenezer Holden, Elizabeth had a child born of her.

D. D. Rex vs. Joshua Simonds & his wife Mary (Badcock), of Windham; Fornication (before marriage); County Court 11 December 1733; WCCCR, vol. 2. Married 27 March 1733; their son Ezekiel Simonds was born 13 June 1733 (WV).

D. D. Rex vs. Jerusha Simons, of Windham; Fornication; County Court June 1748; WCCCR, vol. 6.

D. D. Rex vs. Sarah Smith, of Windham; Fornication; County Court June 1769; WCCCR, vol. 12. Dicey Martin was born to Sarah Smith on 5 January 1769 (WV).

D. D. Rex vs. Mehitable Sparks, of Windham; Fornication; County Court June 1747; WCCCR, vol. 6.

Phebe Stevens, of Windham vs. Joseph Ginnings, of Windham; Maintenance; Writ 1 January 1732; County Court 1732-1733; WCCCR, vol. 2. The Windham vitals lists the birth of Eunice Ginnings, born to Phebe Stevens, 13 July 1732, reputed father Joseph Ginnings.

D. D. Rex vs. David Thomas & his wife Mary (Johnson) Thomas, of Windham; Fornication (before marriage); Writ 17 June 1740; County Court 8 December 1740; WCCCR, vol. 5. David and Mary were married 10 October 1739 (WV). Their daughter Mary Thomas was born 10 April 1740; died 20 May 1741 (WV).

Anne Utely, of Windham vs. Richard King, of Windham; Maintenance; Writ 18 February 1779; County Court December 1778; WCCCR, vol. 15; Anne's child was born 10 June 1779.

D. D. Rex vs. Hannah Utely, of Windham; Fornication; County Court February 1749/50; WCCCR, vol. 6. She may be the daughter of James and Anna Utely born 15 June 1731 (WV).

D. D. Rex vs. Ann, wife of Ichabod Warner, of Windham; Fornication (before marriage); Writ 23 June 1752; WCCCF, box 392.

D. D. Rex vs. Lydia Waters, of Windham; Fornication;
County Court 12 December 1738; WCCCR, vol. 3.

**D. D. Rex vs. Mary (Mudge) Webb, wife of
Napthali/Nathan, of Windham;** Fornication (before marriage); County Court June 1752; WCCCF, box 392.
Napthali/Nathan and Mary were married 2 October 1751; their
daughter was born 27 February 1752. Witnesses to the birth
were: Lydia Silsby; Abigail, wife of John Walden; and Anne,
wife of John Webb, all of Windham.

D. D. Rex vs. Ruth Webb, of Windham; Fornication; County
Court 23 February 1741/42; WCCCR, vol. 5.

**D. D. Rex vs. Timothy & Sarah (Hayward) Webb, of
Windham;** Fornication (before marriage); Writ May 1728;
WCCCF, box 365 (not in records). Timothy and Sarah were
married 26 May 1728 (WV).

**Anna, wife of Solomon Wheat, of Windham vs. John Fitch,
Jr., of Windham;** Fornication; County Court 8 December
1730; WCCCR, vol. 1.

Family Secrets

WOODSTOCK, WINDHAM COUNTY, CT

D. D. Rex vs. Easter Hammond, single woman, of Wood-stock; Fornication; Writ November 1753; County Court 12 December 1753; WCCCF, box 395. The child was born about September 1753, a boy, according to the files. The Woodstock vitals give the date as 28 October 1753, ( )th son of Esther Hammond. Notes in the file indicate that Easter is "dangerously ill" as of 31 January 1754.

DUDLEY, WORCESTER COUNTY, MA

Elizabeth Trumbull, single woman, of Dudley, MA vs. Jonathan Haskell, of Killingly; Maintenance; Writ 17 April 1758; County Court December 1759; WCCCF, box 399. Elizabeth's daughter was born 28 June 1758, according to the files. The Killingly vitals state that Elizabeth's daughter Tamor Haskell was born 29 June 1758 and the reputed father was Jonathan Haskell. Jonathan may be the son of Squire and Elizabeth Haskell born 13 April 1735 (KV). There are also two marriages for Jonathan Haskell in the Killingly vitals.

WARWICK, PROVIDENCE COUNTY, RI

Mary Jeffers, of Warwick, RI vs. Asa Kingsbury, of Plain-field; Maintenance; Writ 12 February 1739/40; County Court 24 June 1740; WCCCR, vol. 4. Asa is probably the son of

Ephraim, Jr., and Lydia Kingsbury born 29 March 1722 (PV). Surety for Asa is Ephraim Kingsbury, of Plainfield.

UNSPECIFIED TOWN

State of Connecticut vs. Jane Cleveland (alias Trumbull); Fornication; County Court August 1785; WCCCR, vol. 16.

D. D. Rex vs. Hannah Herrington; Fornication; County Court June 1771; WCCCR, vol. 12.

State of Connecticut vs. Jane Trumball (alias Cleveland); Fornication; County Court August 1785; WCCCR, vol. 16.

D. D. Rex vs. Mary Wilkinson; Fornication; County Court 26 June 1744; WCCCR, vol. 5. Mary could not pay her fine until Samuel Gray agreed to become her surety. She was bound out to him for a period of one year in order to repay him.

D. D. Rex vs. Jacob Wiley and wife; Fornication (before marriage); County Court 24 June 1725; WCCCR, vol. 2.

* * * * *

-----, Oliver, 58

A

Abbe, Eunice, 74, Eunice (Church), 74, Isaac, 74, Zerviah, 75

Abbitt/Abbott, Esther (Lyon), 1

Abbott, Freelove (Burgess), 75, Mary, 1, Nathaniel, Jr., 1, Stephen, 75

Adams, Constance, 7, Esther, 6, Isaac, 13, 56, Johannah/Hannah, 6, 7, John, 6, Mary, 52, 65

Allen, David, 53, Elizabeth, 10, Joseph, Jr., 75, Lois, 53, Mary, 53, Mehitable, 75, Rebeckah (Robinson), 75

Anderson, Abigail, 46, John, 65

Angell, Samuel, 53

Anne, (an Indian), 42

Arms, Jonathan, 82

Armstrong, Hannah, 28

Arnold, Daniel, 57, 58, Lucy, 58, Robe, 57, 58, Smith, 58

Ashford, Windham Co., CT, 1, 2, 3, 4, 5

Aspinwell, Prince, 48

B

Back, Judah, 77

Backus, Stephen, 6

Bacon, Darius, 64

Badcock, Mary, 85

Baitan, James, 2

Baker, Joel, 53, Lucy, 53, Martha, 76, Nabby/Abigail, 53, Patty, 42

Balch, Dorothy, 42, John, 42, Margaret (Triscott), 42, Zerviah, 43

Baldwin, Ebenezer, 6, Eunice, 13, John, 7, Mary, 7

Barber, Betsey, 49, John, 49

Bartholomew, Hannah, 1

Bartlett, Desire, 28, 29, Ichabod, 29

Bass, Dorothy (Parish), 76, Elizabeth, 75, Henry, 75, Mary, 75, Thomas, 76

Bassett, Dorcas, 20, 43, Nathaniel, Jr., 20, Rufus, 43

Bates, Esther, 7

Bennett, Daniel, 58

Bias, Hannah, 7

Bibbins, Hannah, 43, Philothea, 43

Bill, Eleazer, 39, Elijah, 31, James, Mrs., 41, John, 29, Jonathan, 29, Martha, 29, Mary, 29, Mehitable (Dowey), 29

Billings, William, 74

Bingham, Augustus Wheatlock, 33 Joseph, 85, Joseph, Jr., 85, Martha, 76, Nathaniel, 76, Rachel, 85, Sarah, 85

Bliss, Bethiah, 29, Elias, 29, Hannah, 29, Henry, 29, Zerviah, 29

Borman/Boardman, William, 67, 68, 69, 70, 71, 72, 73

Bosworth, Mehitable, 43

Bourn, Elizabeth, 83

Bowers, John, Jr., 63

Bradford, Lois, 29, 38

Washburn, Elizabeth, 20

Waterford, New London Co., CT, 21, 22

Waters, Lydia, 87

Wattle, Mary, 35

Weaver, Hannah, 73, 74

Webb, Anne, 87, Eunice, 77, Henry, 22, John, 87, Mary (Mudge), 87, Napthali/Nathan, 87, Nathaniel, 79, Ruth, 87, Samuel, 79, Sarah (Hayward), 87, Timothy, 87

Webster, Grace, 41, John, 41, Lester, 76, Lucy, 60, 61, Mary (Dewey), 41

Welch, James, 52, Martha, 52, Mary, 52

Wells, Dorothy, 50, 52

West, Dorothy, 40, Hannah, 40, Jerusha (Hinkley), 40, John, 40, Joshua, 38, Nathan, 40

Westerly, Washington Co., RI, 65

Wheat, Anna, 87, Solomon, 87

Wheeler, Anna (Grosvenor), 56, Josiah, 56, Mary, 56

Whitmore, Abigail, 63, Elizabeth, 26, John, 63, 64, John, Jr., 62

Whitney, David, 52, Elizabeth (Warren), 52, Esther, 52, Eunice, 6, Ezekiel, 52

Wiley, Jacob, 89, Mrs., 89

Wilkinson, Lucy, 14, Mary, 89

Williams, Abigail, 14, Abigail (Knight), 14, Abijah, 40, Daniel, 41, Daniel, Jr., 40,, Elizabeth, 41, Elizabeth (Twogood), 40,

Isaiah, 14, Jehiel, 40, Mary, 41, Moses, 39, William, 37

Willington, Tolland Co., CT, 74

Wilson, Joseph, 5, Laura, 5, Lorry, 5, Mary, 5

Windham, Windham Co., CT, 21, 31, 48, 58, 60, 71, 73, 74, 75, 76, 77, 78, 79, 80, 81, 82, 83, 84, 85, 86, 87

Wise, Grace (Webster), 41, Jonathan, 41, Prudence, 31, Samuel, 41

Woodstock, Windham Co., CT, 6, 88

Woodward, Deliverance, 12, Hannah, 12, John, 12

Wright, Abel, 38, Benjamin, 41, Lucy, 41, Miriam, 38, Rachel, 41, Rebecca, 38, Samuel S., 1, Sarah, 38

www.ingramcontent.com/pod-product-compliance
Lightning Source LLC
Chambersburg PA
CBHW071053090426
42737CB00013B/2340